I0165675

The Bridge

Connecting Violin and Fiddle Worlds

Annemieke Pronker-Coron

Culicidae Press, LLC
918 5th Street
Ames, IA 50010
USA
www.culicidaepress.com

editor@culicidaepress.com

Culicidae
PRESS, LLC
culicidaepress.com

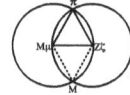

Ames | Gainesville | Lemgo | Rome

Second Edition

THE BRIDGE: CONNECTING VIOLIN AND FIDDLE WORLDS.
Copyright © 2019 by Annemieke Pronker-Coron. All rights
reserved.

For the author's website, go to annemiekecoron.com

No part of this book may be reproduced in any form by any
electronic or mechanized means (including photocopying,
recording, or information storage and retrieval) without written
permission, except in the case of brief quotations embodied in
critical articles and reviews.

For more information, please visit www.culicidaepress.com

ISBN: 978-1-68315-018-3

Cover design and interior layout © 2019 by polytekton.com

Dedication

To the late George E. Custer (1926-2014),
violinist, fiddler, and teacher of both

Table of Contents

Heritage only lives by passing on tradition. If young people are not exposed to the heritage of their culture and country, that heritage may be in danger of dying out.

Annemieke Pronker-Coron

Foreword to the 2019 Edition

Time has passed and new generations of fiddlers spread their wings and share some incredible music varying from gypsy jazz and choro music to Nordic fiddling. Together with my friends Ken and Dana we started hosting these amazing musicians in our home town, Gainesville, as they pass through on their national and international tours. Their concerts and/ or workshops gradually expand the tapestry of music adding rich colors and refinement.

We have been honored with visits by Mike Block, a cellist of the Silk Road Ensemble, with his wife Hanneke, who plays Scottish fiddle. Alasdair Fraser and Natalie Haas are another fiddle-and-cello duo playing top-level Scottish music and teaching their music and the groove in a most exciting workshop. This spring we welcome back Tim Kliphuis, Dutch gypsy jazz violinist with Alfonso Ponticelli on guitar. To top it off, the Nordic Fiddlers Bloc will share their music with us from Norway, the Shetlands and Sweden.

THE FIDDLE BRIDGE

ANDREW FINN MAGILL
5/24/18
FOR ANNEMIEKE PRONKER-
CORON

Thanks again for the wonderful
concert in Gainesville Annemieke!
Here's to "THE BRIDGE"!

Early this year Andrew Finn Magill, "Finn", visited with us. He introduced us to his music. Growing up in Asheville, North Carolina, his first predominant musical style was Irish fiddle music. Learning from the great American and Irish fiddle masters at the Swannanoa Gathering he joined their ranks as a teacher and performer. Fate brought him to Brazil where he was introduced to choro and other great musical styles from there. Finn and his music is exciting and rejuvenating to listen to.

As this book conveys, it is very important to me to help bridge that gap between the different styles of violin and fiddle performance. It matters not what or who we are. Good music outweighs mediocre music and we can enrich our music by learning from other styles of music.

Discussing this topic with these musicians is only natural. And it led to Finn writing a fiddle tune crossing that bridge…a little baroque, some Irish…"The Fiddle Bridge" (see previous page).

Thank you, Finn!

Annemieke Pronker-Coron,
Gainesville, Florida
February 2019

Andrew Finn Magill (fiddle) and Alan Murray (guitar)

Foreword to the 2015 Edition

It takes a lot of courage and desire to follow your heart and chase your dreams. Born in Holland and studying to become a classical violinist, Annemieke Pronker had the courage and desire to follow her interest in learning alternate styles of violin playing.

From her classical background and all her years of playing classically, she still wanted to learn about bluegrass and country and cajun fiddling. She did the right thing and went to where there were good fiddlers. I am certain that others told her she couldn't play multiple styles and do them all well. When I was a young contest fiddler, older fiddlers told me that playing bluegrass would ruin my fiddling. Annemieke didn't listen to those voices, but followed her heart and chased her dream. That takes courage and desire.

I was born in the middle of the U.S. and grew up playing the style of fiddle music my Dad had learned from the local musicians. Every section of the country has a unique fiddle style, sort of their own language you might say. But I believe the most amazing thing about the world of music is that folks from anywhere can learn from each other regardless of the local culture.

I was pleased to learn that Annemieke discovered my fiddling in her home country of Holland. My band, Country Gazette, toured there often and even had a hit record in 1973. When I first met her in Florida, I could tell she had a passion to learn more about "fiddling." I also thought it was cool that she was from Holland.

I am proud of Annemieke for bridging her way into both worlds of fiddling. I believe this book is a must for any player who would like to explore other musical styles, and become more of a well-rounded musician.

Byron Berline

Three-Time National Fiddle Champion

Founder of the Oklahoma International Bluegrass Festival

Member of Bill Monroe and the Bluegrass Boys (1966-1967)

More information at www.doublestop.com

Preface

In musical instrument language a bridge usually refers to the part of the violin that supports the strings and transfers its vibrations to the instrument's body. It conducts the sound as well as the music produced by the player. In a wider sense, however, a bridge is a passage that connects two worlds—in this case the world of the violin and the world of the fiddle.

As a freshly minted classically trained violin teacher in Holland at the beginning of my career, I was naturally trying to become a better teacher and musician. My students were interested in learning to play classical as well as popular music. It troubled me that I was unable to help them learn non-classical music. Due to a personal connection in Gainesville, Florida I decided—while still in the Netherlands—to go to Florida and explore the music culture of fiddling. Thinking that it would enhance my teaching to learn more about fiddling—I had heard it was actively present in the music culture in the southeastern United States—I found incredible connections and explored this new world of fiddling.

Three components formed the foundation for the musical persona that evolved on my journey to the United States and into the fiddle world. I grew up with a mix of classical and popular music, then immersed myself in the baroque and classical violin world at the conservatory, and finally became aware of the importance of improvisation during my music-therapy training. My musical journey to the United States allowed me to realize a great need for sharing my views and experience in the form of this book that intends to shed light on a gap between the classical violin and popular fiddle cultures formed centuries ago, and form a bridge uniting these two worlds. In these pages I share my views on the importance to bridge that gap by learning about the roots of both cultures as well as the commonalities and differences between them.

The Gap And The Bridge

Typically fiddlers refer to classical violinists as musicians using a completely different technique than their own, e.g. the use of long-drawn bows and vibrato are main pillars of the classical approach. At the very beginning of my journey I was shown some of the main characteristics of old-time fiddling i.e., shorter bow strokes, relaxed bow arm, circular bow movement, and occasional swing strokes. I was excited to discover that these fiddle techniques in the United States were directly linked to baroque violin technique with which I was so familiar from my studies in the Netherlands.

This realization encouraged me to take a closer look at the history of violin and fiddle music in order to find perhaps a common ground. In Europe, during the Renaissance era (1450-1600), a gap started to develop between the fiddle music in taverns and the music played at the courts. At first the gap was not very apparent because dance music was featured in both venues. However, gradually the music world began to divide into two streams, namely popular and classical music. During the Baroque era (1600-1750) more formal compositions, such as the suite (a collection of dances), became common at the courts. An aural tradition continued among folk musicians. The gap widened. Both fiddle and violin worlds developed virtuoso techniques. New styles evolved in the popular realm, like jazz and bluegrass. Violin solos composed by Nicolo Paganini and "Fritz" (Friedrich) Kreisler were filled with virtuoso grandstands, and romantic violin concertos displayed, arguably, the most technically complex cadenzas. The gap between violinists and fiddlers continued to widen.

Today professional training academies no longer focus only on classical music. Violinists and fiddlers explore different styles. Take Mark O'Connor, for example, who is a great American fiddler building bridges between bluegrass, jazz, classical, and other music as he creates fiddle concertos and other cross-style-based compositions. In 2009 he launched his violin method that covers American music and bridges the gap. This movement is encouraging. It appears that now is a wonderful time to learn more about the roots and developments of violin and fiddle performance.

Sharing A Musical Journey

I would like to invite you to travel together on a journey. This book will help the reader better understand why it is important to explore beyond the known extent of one's violin or fiddle style of playing and teaching. It shares stories to which you may relate, and consists of experiences on a journey leading to realizations that hopefully brings musicians, whether beginner or advanced, closer to their desire to bridge the gap.

One day I had the great honor to host master fiddler Byron Berline. He and several others were sharing their recordings in an intimate setting. I was excited to be part of a lively conversation and asked the group to listen to a recorded piece that I had performed with my Greek band. Byron commented. "Did you use sheet music?" He was right. My excitement was suddenly dampened by a new insight. The track with my solo, well enough liked by my colleagues, was missing certain qualities of freedom and imagination that would have been present by way of improvisation. Experienced musicians like Berline were able to recognize the lack of improvisation and hear the connection to the actual sheet music in the recording. Berline and fiddlers like him are masters of improvisation. A tune like this one would definitely be enhanced by some freedom—along with an audible increase in speed—to bring out the exciting qualities of the music.

My approach is that of a violinist from Europe seeking to bridge this gap, starting in the violin world and reaching out to the fiddle world. I believe that violinists and fiddlers alike have a strong sense of knowing just what the other world is about. Assumptions and sometimes very strong statements are made regarding the musicians 'on the other side'. For me this is accompanied with a certain sense of discomfort since my personal journey gave me a great opportunity to witness the incredible beauty of music in both worlds. Yet it became clear how the gap, formed centuries ago, has not disappeared.

It is the lack of knowledge of the other world that widens this gap. It is natural to hold on to what we know best, our own way of playing the instrument. We expand the gap when we feel the other way of playing represents a threat to our own. Yet we need not see that other way of playing as a style that will supplant ours. It is the exploration of that other territory, and learning more about it, that will give us the opportunity to enrich and deepen our musicianship.

I have come to believe that we can learn to play both fiddle and violin in their distinctly different styles. We can teach a comprehensive approach right from the start. We don't even need different instruments. Instead, we need an appreciation for and an understanding of the depth of the styles we want to play. I hope you enjoy my explorations and find this book food for thought—and maybe for action—to join me in bridging the gap between the violin and fiddle culture.

This book is for violin educators, violin and fiddle students who would like to teach and perform, and fiddlers who are curious to learn more about the connection of the fiddle heritage with the European baroque and classical world. It bridges a gap that I have witnessed between the world of violinists and fiddlers, a gap that was formed centuries ago. Fear of possibly being influenced in technique and artistry seems to lie behind the utterances of each group about the other group. Each group appears to hold up high their conviction that the other group has no clue how to play in their style. With this book I hope to encourage both worlds to consider exploring the other in order to enrich their own musicianship. I hope to find common ground and understanding by exploring common roots.

Principles I Would Like To Convey

- Whether you call yourself a violinist or a fiddler, your art has value, not less or more than the other.
- The violin and fiddle are the same instrument and share their roots.
- For both baroque violin and fiddle technique, elements of performance and idiom are similar.
- We can learn from the other music style and enrich our own way of music making.
- Violin educators can teach and introduce fiddling and different styles of music to their students without needing to be expert in the field.
- It is important to connect to the desire of the student – what music do they favor and what music is part of their heritage.
- It is important not to see classical music as separate from all other music. It does not stand alone and is enriched by practicing elements of other styles.
- By understanding the connection, no matter the style we play, we will improve our musicianship by exploring beyond our own style.
- Violinists can learn to play fiddle and fiddlers can learn to play violin – if they desire and choose to learn and immerse themselves in the other world.
- Forming bridges opens the road to letting go of ignorance. Both violin and fiddle music will have more chance to survive and flourish.

For the Fiddler

- A fiddler might be curious due to "what is there to bridge?" due to my story and due to the fiddlers/musicians they recognize.
- A fiddler might learn that what they think is technique unique to fiddling is closely related to baroque violin technique.
- A fiddler can learn that it is ok to work on technical aspects with a violinist, within the field of baroque technique and beyond.

For the Classically Trained Violinist

- Classically trained violinists who teach and perform can learn fiddle vocabulary, methods, literature, and about virtuoso fiddlers' creative lives.
- They could learn that fiddling is not as different as they think, and there is a way to learning the fiddle feel.
- The importance of learning from other musical styles and the way they are played.
- A road towards how to learn improvisation and where to explore…e.g. Mark O'Connor.
- How important and enriching it is for one's own music to go outside the box.

For the Baroque Violinist

- Baroque violinists could learn that their technique is not unique to baroque music and that especially old-time fiddlers share similar roots.
- They could learn that in order to become better *baroque* musicians, they would be helped by exploring other musical styles such as fiddling.

This book will guide you from personal experiences to observations and realizations to a philosophy of reaching out and bridging the gap between violin and fiddle music.

Overview of the Book

Chapter 1: My Musical Journey: Learning to Play Fiddle takes you on a journey with me, a classically educated European violinist who studied with a virtuoso Dutch baroque violinist, into the world of fiddling in the United States. I share observations and experiences that form the basis for understanding the importance to bridge musical worlds.

Chapter 2: Comparing Baroque Violin and Fiddle Performance Practice explores shared roots in dance, and commonalities of playing techniques during the seventeenth and eigthteenth centuries in Europe and the art of fiddling.

Chapter 3 The World of Fiddlers includes insightful tips from four internationally known virtuoso fiddlers.

Chapter 4: Building Bridges: Connections Between Baroque, Classical-Romantic, and Fiddling Performance Practice compares and contrasts similarities and differences of violin and fiddle culture, instruments, technique, vocabulary, and musicians.

In Chapter 5: Moving Forward: The Teacher's Role :Turning Experience Into Philosophy explores how we may overcome obstacles and build bridges so as to encourage a rich heritage continue to flourish in future generations.

Chapter 1
My Musical Journey:
Learning to Play Fiddle

Amsterdam

During the course of our lives it seems inevitable that we interweave our personal stories with our professional ones. I, too, cannot separate the two. My choices in life led from an early career in classical violin teaching and performance in Europe, to a world of fiddling and continuation of classical violin performance in the southeastern United States.

In the late 1980s my hometown was the Dutch city of Amsterdam. In 1984 I completed my studies at the Sweelinck Conservatory (Conservatorium van Amsterdam). Expected levels of performance were high and very competitive. I was proud to attend this prestigious academy with my main focus on violin instruction, and was very fortunate to have studied there with baroque violinist Jaap Schröder. His teaching of early music has influenced me greatly.

After graduating in 1984 I began an odyssey to find a direction in my musical life. At the conservatory I had learned how to play the violin well and how to teach it. However, this appeared not enough to satisfy my restless mind. I was eager to learn more about the musical world and the tremendous effect music has on people in many different ways. In 1990 my music explorations led me to the United States where I instinctively understood that my previous experiences and desire to learn would be well answered in the world of fiddling.

During my training at the conservatory I took a course in music therapy and became intrigued by the tremendous power of music, both as a language and a means toward therapeutic ends. I explored the option of studying to become a music therapist, visited several institutions, and took brief courses in the Netherlands. I learned about an excellent one-year intensive course in Wimbledon, England at the Southlands College of the Roehampton Institute of Higher Education. Indeed, not long after graduating from the conservatory, I wrote a grant in order to study music therapy at this institution, and was accepted into the program. It was an intensive year devoted to learning about the enormous effect music has on children with special needs, including autism and cerebral palsy. I learned about the great importance of being in touch with the basic beat in each of us. We all have a different tempo or beat by which we live. Getting in touch with that beat can be very powerful and can help us find a balance and live more fully.

However, on my return to the Netherlands I didn't become a music therapist. My improvisation skills were too limited and I was not able to use them sufficiently within a therapy setting. No matter how excellent the courses at the conservatory, and no matter the high standard of playing and theoretical understanding of music, the freedom of expression found in improvisation was a skill that didn't come easy for me. Instead I had been very focused on exact directions regarding general performance technique such as bowing, fingering, and articulation, as well as being very attentive to the exploration of the musical expression as intended by composers.

I studied one more year at the conservatory, built up my teaching practice and tried to get as many orchestra engagements as I could manage, slowly building up a teaching practice in Amsterdam as well as in the neighboring city of Haarlem. It wasn't a great income but I could sustain myself well. Then, gradually, it became clear to me that a number of my students showed interest in playing non-classical music, yet I didn't quite know how to respond to that request. How could I keep my students interested in music and in playing the violin if their wish was to look beyond the classical world? Rock, jazz and other popular musical styles were high on their list of favorites.

Fully classically trained, I found it practically impossible to answer that demand. I had no idea how to even start teaching rock music. Jazz would be quite difficult, particularly because of its chord structure, complex rhythms, and intricate rules of improvisation. Besides feeling unequipped to teach these different styles of music, I was thrown back to the question of improvisation. It was pivotal in my attempt to become a music therapist and now this aspect of music making was looming again.

One day in Amsterdam I met Ron Wallace, an American professor from Orlando, Florida. My interest piqued when he shared that there were people in Florida who played fiddle. He assured me there were jam sessions and bluegrass festivals to attend. I happened to know someone near Gainesville, Florida. I started to see a possibility of new explorations, even if traveling to the United States was a big decision. However, having a friend in the area and realizing Gainesville was a university town gave me the courage to go. I figured that I would be able to tap into university resources. I immediately started to develop my idea of spending four months in the U.S. doing research in bluegrass fiddling.

Byron Berline and the *Country Gazette*

Interior of the music store Concerto *in Amsterdam*

There was one hurdle, however. I needed to find out how bluegrass fiddling sounded, so I visited a record store, searching for examples of bluegrass music. The salesman took me to the records with the heading "Country Music" and showed me a record called *Country Gazette*. I was confused since it hadn't occurred to me that fiddling had any connection with country music. He assured me this was bluegrass. In the Netherlands, American country music wasn't very popular, as far as I knew. I realized how little I knew about fiddling, country, and bluegrass music. I saw a fiddler on the cover, so I gathered there would be some fiddling on this record.

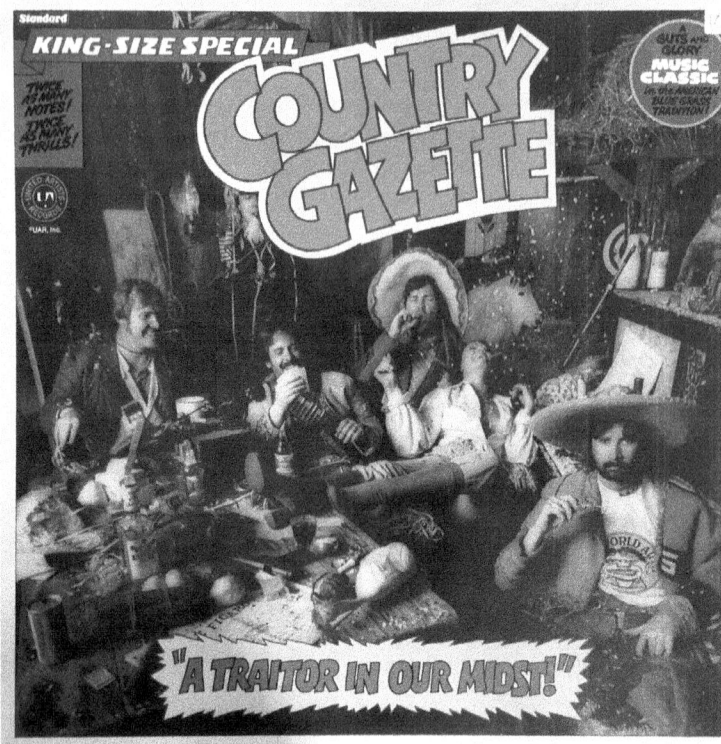

Country Gazette record cover

I couldn't believe my ears! The fiddling was incredible! The tempo was fast and upbeat. It sounded accessible, yet complex. There was much to learn and a wide open world, waiting to be explored. If this was fiddling, I wanted to be on the next flight to the United States. I listened to this record day and night and was completely overwhelmed by the phenomenal musicianship of this fiddler, whose name was Byron Berline.

I didn't quite catch the next plane to the United States. Things never are all that straightforward. My requests for grants were turned down and my savings were inadequate. However, at the Dutch musicians' organization, the Koninklijke Nederlandse Toonkunstenaars Vereniging (KNTV) in Amsterdam, I was welcomed by a remarkable woman, Juut van Waveren, who listened patiently to my story and provided instruction. She was a key figure in shaping my plan and putting it in motion. With her help I was able to secure a loan which provided the resources to go to the United States and research bluegrass fiddling on a private basis.

Gainesville, 1990

Before I left Amsterdam, my Gainesville friend Larry Ash sent an itinerary that included the name and location of Sabine, a local music store, so I could make connections and learn about the music scene in town. Once in Florida, I connected with the music department at the University of Florida and auditioned for the Gainesville Chamber Orchestra. This way I surrounded myself with people in my professional field and created a support system while exploring a new culture very foreign to me. I was excited but didn't really know what to expect.

First Experiences with Live Bluegrass Music

Wednesday night jam session in Gainesville:
George Custer, Mac McClung and Lance Lazonby

Within my first week in Gainesville I went to a Wednesday night jam session. Hesitantly, I brought my violin. What could I possibly play or do with no sheet music in sight? Both panic and excitement came over me. Indeed, that night I was the focus of the party as the other jam session musicians provided me with tunes that they believed I could play. They played famous songs like *House of the Rising Sun* and *Summertime*, among others. There was bluegrass music, too. I learned that "taking a break" means to play solo. When I heard "Anna, take it!" my heart stood still and I broke into a sweat. I played some notes, especially long ones, but my fingers wouldn't really move properly since

I had no clue yet about "licks", those short phrases that are at the heart of bluegrass music. I had no idea of the underlying chords, and played loudly as I stumbled my way through.

I never refused when offered to "play a break". That night there were guitar players, fiddlers, a banjo and bass player as well as a mandolin player. For the first time I saw and heard bluegrass music played informally as part of a jam session. I was thrilled! Until then I had played only with classical musicians. It was the first time I made music together with people playing these instruments. The bass was familiar, of course, yet the strings were plucked and slapped. The mandolin looked different because, unlike the round bottom instrument I had seen in Europe, bluegrass musicians used a flat-bottomed mandolin. The way it was played was very exciting, nothing like I had ever heard before. And I was utterly intrigued by the amazing sound of the banjo. The guitars were really the most familiar to me, though I do not believe I had ever played with guitar backup before. A new world opened and it was incredible!

That night I had taken only a little peek into this new world. The music was predominantly bluegrass, with some classic rock and swing. I heard *some* fiddling as the night progressed, but not really any specific fiddle tunes. There was so much yet to learn.

Not All Fiddling is Bluegrass

Fay Baird (old-time banjo; open-backed) at a jam session in Gainesville, Florida, 2015 (image courtesy of Mikesch Muecke)

A week later I was introduced to a different style of fiddling namely "old-time" music. Not all fiddling in the United States is bluegrass music. An old-time jam session made me realize the many different styles of fiddling that are actively played, including bluegrass, old-time, Irish fiddling, Cajun fiddling, and Texas Swing music. That week I went to my second jam session in the area and met many new people. Only a few of the musicians of the previous week attended. The place was filled with fiddlers, sitting in an informal circle in the room. They were joined by some guitar and mandolin players, and by a banjo player who played differently from the one the previous week. This was clawhammer style banjo, unlike the bluegrass banjo the week before. The sound was very different. It was gentler due to the open backed body and the strumming rather than picking of strings. It suited the overall sound of the old-time music quite well.

Old-Time Fiddlers

Willie Jones, old-time fiddle (image courtesy of Humberto Herrera)

Tom Staley, Fay Baird, and Annemieke Pronker-Coron at a jam session at the Florida State Fiddlers Convention, 1991

The fiddlers held their instruments in a wide variety of ways. I was surprised to see that they actually could get a decent sound out of their instruments, despite these postures. The musicians held the bows in different places along the bow, and not necessarily at the frog. The instruments typically were held slanted down towards the ground in some relaxed fashion. The use of shoulder-rests appeared to be highly unpopular and the fiddlers seemed to prefer tiny bow strokes as they played their tunes.

I sat next to a very friendly fiddler who immediately tried to help me. I turned my tape recorder on and prior to every tune he announced the name of the tune, e.g., *Golden Slippers*. To my amazement, the tune wouldn't stop! The relatively short melody was played many times over and over.

The Aural Tradition: A New Experience

For the first time I tried to learn to play a tune by watching the other fiddlers, following their fingers, looking at the bow, listening to the sound, and trying to figure out where the melody was going. As long as I could figure out what string(s) they were playing, I had a starting point. Having never done this before, I found it daunting. That first night I did not pick up much by way of this method, which for fiddlers is the common way of sharing and learning new tunes following an aural tradition.

The aural tradition consists of the direct transmission of musical culture from person to person. For example, in the Appalachian Mountains before the introduction of mechanical recording, this was the popular way of passing on tunes to one another. Most musicians were unable to read notated or sheet-music and relied instead on this mode of personal instruction and social connection. This process within the folk-traditions is inherent in what people refer to as "old-time." As a result, "old-time" fiddle tunes are played in many different renditions that can vary quite substantially from the original tune.

Being somewhat overwhelmed with trying to pick up the tunes this way, I began to relax and tried to find harmonies that sounded good with the melody. These I played along with the melody, while trying to match the style of bowing and the music's feel or character.

The fiddlers all played the tune together which produced a colorful mixed sound since everyone had their own way of playing it. Not only might they have different bow strokes, or a slightly different timing, but the notes themselves might be a myriad of variations on the original tune. The goal was not to sound uniform, like one might expect from a violin section in an orchestra, but to sound authentic and to create an original "in-the moment" tune. The lightness and spontaneity of the fiddling melded the sound into a very special blend of music, a layering of renditions.

I felt transported into a different space where music was played and enjoyed by all present with shared excitement. This was a style of music and way of playing together that I had never experienced before. I could tell there were unspoken rules I had yet to learn, but it was very inclusive and inviting. Within moments I felt that I had become member of the group.

Recording Jam Sessions and
Studying Fiddle and Violin

Soon I started to fill my days with listening to tapes, including the ones I recorded at jam sessions. I was told to immerse myself in this fiddle music, so I went to jam sessions and festivals, and explored the licks and tunes that I heard performed. Up to now I had never tried to learn by listening to music, without access to notes on paper. To pick up what was played on the tapes seemed completely impossible. As soon as I thought I heard some notes, they were gone before I could translate them on my violin. I was told there are special devices that slow down music, yet don't change the pitch. However, I had no access to such devices. I also explored some of the fiddle books I purchased, trying to figure out what sections were good for me to learn. That was not easy either as the books that were on the market at the time had directions that seemed somewhat scattered and didn't mean much to me.

While my roommate was out, I practiced in the apartment, but for serious study I would go to the music department at the University of Florida and find a practice room. There I practiced what I knew, e.g., scales, sonatas, concertos, and études. Without more direction in fiddling, I was lost.

George E. Custer (1926-2014)

George Custer and Annemieke Pronker–Coron,
Florida Folk Festival in White Springs, 1998

Clearly I needed some help. A fiddle teacher would be just the thing. I had asked the violin professor at the University of Florida and also inquired at the jam session. Everyone directed me to George Custer who lived in the town of Salt Springs in Marion County, about an hour's drive from Gainesville. I only had a bicycle. Having traveled thousands of miles to learn about bluegrass fiddling, I realized that this highly recommended teacher lived just out of my reach. I called anyway and found a most delightful man who appeared willing to meet and hear my story. A banjo player and friend, Michael Peyton, drove me to Salt Springs where George and I met, talked, played, and talked some more. He showed me tunes, licks, and ways to practice. George agreed to teach me every other week and Michael drove me there—a true friend. I recorded the lessons on audio cassette and learned a lot. George showed me fiddle techniques and listened carefully to my classical approach. Since he also played violin in the regional orchestra, the classical way of playing was familiar to him. I learned to play fiddle tunes that were some of his favorites. These included *Faded Love, Tennessee Blues, Big Sandy River, Blackberry Blossom*, and *Jerusalem Ridge*, to name a few. Soon I was well on my way to getting a better idea and feel about bluegrass fiddling. George was invaluable on my fiddle journey. It was a privilege to be his student.

Bluegrass Festivals and the Soggy Bottom Bluegrass Bunch

Using my bicycle was limiting because it wouldn't take me far, but again I was fortunate. My friend Michael drove me to all kinds of places farther afield which allowed me to attend a number of bluegrass festivals in the area. It was at one such event that I met the Soggy Bottom Bluegrass Bunch, a club of enthusiastic pickers who played together at jam sessions and gathered on the campgrounds at bluegrass festivals.

During the festival weekend they would pick music together throughout the night and into the early morning hours. I was welcomed warmly into their midst, invited into their jam sessions, and given 'breaks'. Often a bottle of whiskey or moonshine was passed around, and I never refused, receiving immediate respect from the pickers.

Initially bluegrass was to me like a foreign language on my violin. Here I was struggling to be understood on the instrument, using my knowledge of music and of playing the violin. My way of playing music did not connect easily with these musicians. I found myself in a world of music that welcomed me, but used a completely different way and style of playing with different rules for musical communication.

As a stranger to this world I tried to listen and learn their ways of playing. What did gradually emerge were some tentative notes, melody lines, as well as some rhythmic patterns. To me these sounded elementary and quite clumsy, but in the bluegrass jam circles I found warm encouragement and compliments for trying. This encouraged me to keep going.

Holding Back

One night Michael Peyton and I attended another fun jam session with the Soggy Bottom Bluegrass Bunch. Michael quietly took me to the side and told me that there were some typical mistakes I made and that sometimes I was actually disruptive to the jam session. In my enthusiasm and eager attempts to join in I had not noticed this. He pointed out two seemingly simple rules related to the etiquette of a jam session.

> *Rule One: When playing along with guitars, it is essential to be really careful not to overpower them when they take their 'break'. A sustained violin sound can easily do that.*

> *Rule Two: When backing up a singer, avoid playing in the singer's vocal range. In this case, the violin's sustained sound can easily cover the voice.*

I learned that I needed to work hard on holding back and not just belting out sound. I had to be more careful when playing long notes so as to not drown out the other musicians. Of course I wished to enhance and not disrupt the fun of making music together. However, in my classical training I had really not worked on these musical elements in the same manner. Thus I was unprepared and unable to react appropriately to these requests. I had learned how to work out musical phrasing and accompanying styles in ensemble playing with written music. The notes and directions provided on the sheet music, such as articulation and dynamics, carefully prescribe or suggest in detail the nature of the accompaniment to the melody. To ascertain and deduce melody from accompaniment in classical compositions was second nature to me. Although I understood what to do, it was very difficult for me to immediately adhere to the rules of 'backup' while improvising in these jam sessions.

The Need for Immersion

Now that I was made aware of the musical requirements to play effectively and with appropriate etiquette in jam sessions, I had to apply myself. The realization of this aspect of playing bluegrass music made it clear to me that there was a lot more to becoming a fiddler and to learning the skills of improvisation than one might think. I needed more occasions for practice. So, I attended more festivals and immersed myself in jam sessions and listening opportunities.

Jam session at a bluegrass festival in Florida,
1990, with Michael Peyton on banjo

The festivals were fun! In addition to wandering around the campgrounds and joining jam sessions, there was the stage area where one could listen throughout the weekend to a packed program of a variety of bands. During these festivals I had the pleasure of hearing some of the best bluegrass musicians.

At one such festival I happened to listen to Robert Russell (aka Chubby Wise). For many years Chubby was the fiddler in Bill Monroe's band, the Bluegrass Boys. He was one of the members of this band when it was referred to as "the original bluegrass band," together with Bill Monroe, Earl Scruggs, Lester Flatt and Howard Watts.

Chubby Wise and Annemieke Pronker-Coron at a
bluegrass festival in Waldo, Florida, 1991

Listening to Chubby play made me feel like I was at the heart of the fiddle world. At the festivals, Chubby would never play a set without performing the famous tune *The Orange Blossom Special.* He repeatedly and rhythmically moved the bow away from the bridge and back towards it, imitating the sound of a train engine. His long beard danced on and off the chin rest as he constantly moved his head. At the bridge of his fiddle, under the strings, I could see a lot of rosin. A classical musician wouldn't dream of being seen with any rosin on the instrument. Yet fiddlers appeared to believe it gave extra flavor to their music. I was fascinated!

Listening to the tapes of the jam sessions and festival performances and to the suggestions I heard from other musicians and the instructions of George Custer, it became clear to me that some of the elements I would have to work on were learning "licks" (short phrases), understanding the chord structure of the songs, and playing appropriate back-up to other musicians.

One way of playing backup was a rhythmic chop of the chord with the bow at the frog, on the "back beat" or "off beat." I learned that a "chop" with the bow on the strings is not so much a bow stroke, but rather a vertical drop of the bow onto the strings, more aimed at providing a slapping, rhythmic sound rather than a beautiful tone. The chop was used often in bluegrass music and was new to me. My sense of rhythm was tested. It seemed that these musicians had an impeccable sense of rhythm and would keep it up tightly. They began with a steady tempo that gradually increased in speed as the tune developed. Rubato was definitely not in the cards.

The instant knowledge of licks in the right keys and chords were an obvious help, but how to acquire that knowledge was the big issue. Thus far, my fingers would freeze and cause me to play long notes rather than licks. My challenge was to find a way to go about learning licks and chords so they would become second nature to me. I was accustomed to practicing the violin for long hours every day, perfecting scales, technique, studies, and classical repertoire. I was very dependent on sheet music. I followed patterns exactly and did not step away from the given sheet music directions. How was I to move to the free interpretation and creation within improvisation?

How Does One Pick Up a Tune Without Sheet Music?

Local group Slow Jam *at the Florida State Fiddlers Convention in Alachua, Florida, 1991*

I attended Slow Jam sessions where beginning fiddlers and other instrumentalists would gather to play fiddle tunes in a slow tempo. This proved to be a great way for me to learn to play fiddle tunes via the aural tradition. I heard and played some fun tunes including *Nail the Catfish to the Tree,* a tune filled with syncopated motives and phrases. Once written down, it seemed infinitely more complicated than when it was just learned by ear, another surprising discovery!

I learned to play more fiddle tunes with George Custer and started to share these at jam sessions. It was exciting to delve more deeply into the world of fiddling. It had become clear to me that four months was not enough time to learn about fiddling and the different styles of playing it. Therefore I requested an extension of my visa with the Immigration and Naturalization Service (INS). With a bit of luck I was able to extend my stay for two more months during which I made a documentary film about bluegrass fiddling.

Making the Video *Bluegrass, an Introduction*

Deciding to create a film about bluegrass fiddling was easy. Making the movie, though, was another story. Mac Rutan, a filmmaker, taught me what to do when filming and how to put together the different elements needed to make a documentary. Alhough I lacked a good audio recording device I did not let that stop me. Mac agreed that it might be ok if I used my portable audio-cassette recorder with a small separate microphone. It would not be perfect, but it would certainly give me an opportunity to make this project happen.

Meanwhile I read whatever materials I could find on fiddling. Together with several interviews and conversations with the musicians around me, I found enough background information to write a script. I recorded jam sessions, concerts, and festivals, as well as musicians by themselves, and put it all together into one master script. Then I took it to Mac, who helped produce it as a one-hour documentary entitled *Bluegrass, an Introduction*. We worked intensely for a week in his studio. I barely saw daylight! We finished the project the day before I flew back to the Netherlands. This was a wonderful product to take home and share with my students in the Netherlands.

The Peyton Brothers at the Thomas Center in Gainesville. My opening shot in the video Bluegrass an Introduction, *1991*

I am proud of *Bluegrass an Introduction,* telling the story of bluegrass music as seen through the eyes of a wandering violinist from Europe. It featured both old-time and bluegrass jam sessions with the local bluegrass band the Peyton Brothers, Chubby Wise playing the *Orange Blossom Special* at the Waldo Bluegrass Festival, George Custer, Aubrey Haynie (fellow student of George Custer), and many others.

Byron Berline

Byron Berline and The Doo Wah Riders (Lindy Rasmusson on guitar) at Disney Pleasure Island, Orlando, Florida, 1991

Byron Berline was a fiddler with *The Country Gazette* band whose record was my introduction to fiddling and my ultimate motivation for this adventure. Since that record I have acquired more of his recordings and continue to be excited about Byron's fiddling. During one of my fiddle lessons with George Custer I said, "You know, I have learned so much and it is really an experience beyond my wildest dreams. Too bad though this country is so vast, as I am sure I will never get to meet my absolute favorite fiddler, Byron Berline." Unbelievably, George told me that Byron was performing close by in Orlando with The Doo Wah Riders band. Incredible! Life somehow has wonderful surprises in store, and here was mine. There was no time to waste and, with some help, I was able to head to Orlando to hear him perform.

Byron Berline and Annemieke Pronker-Coron at Disney
Pleasure Island, Orlando, Florida, 1991

That night in Orlando I didn't hear much bluegrass fiddle music since The Doo Wah Riders fit more into the country rock than bluegrass category. They played electric, which was quite different from the many acoustic bands I had heard so far. I also noticed how one can play electric fiddle with sound effects in ways I had never seen or heard before. Byron had a little box with a foot pedal, which changed the sound substantially while he played. He was indeed the virtuoso I had imagined. When the band took a break, I took the opportunity to speak with him. I learned that he did not teach, but was willing to show me more about his playing style. He also offered to answer any questions I had about fiddle playing.

Indeed, a few days later, I was able to sit down with Byron for a few hours. He showed me one tune or lick after another. Even though I couldn't understand it all, I knew how valuable that time was with him. Listening to that recording now still gives me great pointers about fiddling. Bluegrass and any other kind of fiddle music really is an incredibly rich world to explore.

From Byron I learned interesting new insights about bowing. Upon his request, I played *Paddy on the Turnpike*, a tune I had learned and played at jam sessions and with bluegrass musicians. I played it so frequently that I was up to a fair speed, but I was nervous playing it for Byron. So I stumbled and didn't recover. I stumbled because the bowing pattern I used was new to me. The bow stroke called "Georgia bow" or "Georgia shuffle" gives the tune a punch by accentuating the off or back-beat. I had learned the tune from sheet music and worked, not only on the notes, but also on an exact reproduction of the suggested bowing. I was eager to learn the secret of the "fiddle feel" and the way fiddlers bow. However, I used my traditional way of learning music by exactly following the written notation. I was stuck.

Byron shared with me that I needed to pay less attention to the bow direction or exact bow strokes. He shared with me that he could not imagine himself to be part of an orchestra where indeed all play exactly the same bowing. I can well understand. He advised me to loosen up my bowing. Since then I have done so. Now I add the "Georgia shuffle" freely, without planning. I have learned to "feel" the music and bow accordingly.

In April 1991 I returned to Amsterdam with a large amount of newly acquired knowledge and experience. Thanks to my many friends I was able to participate in jam sessions, watch concerts, and visit festivals as well as take fiddle lessons. Also, thanks to these many new friends, I was able to create a video documentary about bluegrass fiddling, giving me something I would be able to take home and share with my students and other interested musicians. I had experienced an absorbing six months that changed my musical life.

Chapter 2
Comparing Baroque Violin
and Fiddle Performance Practice

Witnessing old-time fiddling at a jam session in 1991 in Florida, my eyes were opened! In a flash, I saw rich overlapping circles. Familiar baroque performance techniques were applied to play old-time fiddling. Old-time fiddling, I realized has its roots in music that was popular in Europe during the Baroque era (1600-1750) and was brought along with the settlers to the United States.

In early music, violin music was performed in two particularly distinctive settings. There was music for church (sacred music), and music for the courts or in villages, taverns and homes (secular music). Focusing on secular dance music, I will compare the essential elements of baroque technique and provide examples of those elements used in fiddle playing.

Jaap Schröder and Annemieke Pronker-Coron in Gainesville, Florida, 1994

My experience has guided me to be a bridge builder. I actively make connections between training at the conservatory in Amsterdam, my experience as a professional classically trained musician, and the world of fiddling. I feel I have grown as a teacher and am able to give my students a more all-round education. I have built bridges by way of my personal training and experience.

At the Sweelinck Conservatorium of Amsterdam I was taught baroque performance technique by world-renowned baroque specialist and violinist Jaap Schröder. Through his teaching I learned how important it is to approach every musical style in its own way, using different violin techniques. This was the starting point and baggage I took with me on my journey to the fiddle world. I still remember my incredible amazement witnessing my first old-time fiddle jam session. Here I was, thousands of miles away from my school and home base, seeing baroque violin technique in action as the featured way to play old-time fiddle music. I started making links and felt an immediate connection to the baroque violin technique. Suddenly I felt closer to the fiddle world and saw a tremendous opportunity for bridging gaps. Since that time I have worked on finding parallels between the violin and fiddle techniques, and in particular the baroque violin technique.

Although I was educated as a classical violinist, my specialty has become baroque violin. I perform professionally with a baroque trio, the Alachua Consort, that specializes in seventeenth and eighteenth-century European repertoire.[1] I feel fortunate and enriched that I was given a chance to learn to play in the baroque style.

---

[1] The Alachua Consort, www.alachuaconsort.com, accessed May 5, 2015

The Alachua Consort: Annemieke Pronker-Coron – violin, John Netardus – oboe, and Miriam Zach – harpsichord (image courtesy of Mikesch Muecke)

Modes

Modes (scales) are ordered series of pitches with a tonic (first tone) as reference point. Different modes have different intervals that are referred to as scale degrees in relation to the tonic reference point.[2]

Modes were used to create music during the Medieval and Renaissance periods in Europe, e.g. , a collection of Renaissance dances in *Het derde musyck boexken* (1551) by Tielman Susato (c. 1510-after 1570).

---

[2] The Editors of Encyclopædia Britannica, *Church modes - Ecclesiastical Mode,* Encyclopedia Britannica: http://www.britannica.com/EBchecked/topic/117215/church-mode, accessed May 7, 2015.

Church Modes

with no sharps or flats
space between brackets are half steps

Church Modes (image courtesy of Annemieke Pronker-Coron)

Many fiddle tunes are written in modes, especially Irish and old-time tunes.[3] Popular modes, include the Mixolydian, Dorian and Aeolian. These modes each have a flatted seventh which gives the popular blues effect. Both the Dorian and Aeolian modes

---

[3] David Brody, *The Fiddler's Fake Book*, Oak Publications, 1983.

have a flatted or minor third, giving the mode a minor character. The names of 'major' and 'minor' refer to the interval 'third' at the beginning of each scale—a major third and a minor third. The distance between the first and third notes gives the mode or scale its major or minor feel.

The Ionian mode became what is referred to as the major scale.

The Dorian mode sounds minor. It has a flatted (minor) third, and major sixth scale degree.

The Mixolydian mode sounds like the Ionian mode (= major scale) until the seventh tone of the scale which is lowered a half step.

The Aeolian mode sounds like (and became) the pure minor scale.

Examples of Fiddle Tunes in Various Modes

Mode	Characteristics	Name of Tune	Type
Dorian	flatted third raised sixth flatted seventh	Drowsy Maggie Frosty Morning The Swallow Tail Jig	Irish Reel Old-Time Irish Jig
Mixolydian	like Major but flatted seventh	June Apple	Old-Time
Aeolian	= pure minor; flatted third flatted seventh	Jerusalem Ridge The King of the Fairies Lonesome Fiddle Blues The Star of the County Down	Bluegrass Irish Bluegrass Irish Ballad/ Waltz

Dance Music: Gigue and Jig

In dance music during the Renaissance and early Baroque eras, violinists focused on rhythm, improvised, and played without sheet music. Later baroque chamber music regularly included dances such as the courante, allemande, and gigue composed and collected into suites or partitas e.g. J.S. Bach's Six *Solo Sonatas and Partitas for Violin*. The form of each dance movement was binary, meaning it had two sections that were repeated. This relates to fiddle music, which bases its heritage on dance music and uses the binary format for the vast majority of its tunes.

A great example is the gigue, which compares to the jig in Irish fiddling. In addition to being popular in Ireland, jigs can be found in Scottish and English fiddling, as well as in North American-Canadian and old-time fiddling. Both the gigue and the jig are lively dances, usually in six-eighth meter. In baroque music, it is typically the last movement of a suite.

The history of the jig and gigue is fascinating, demonstrating how early baroque music was intertwined with fiddling. The jig may have originated in England in the 1500s and spread to Ireland where it was very popular. The actual place of origin is uncertain. Andrew Kuntz in the *Fiddler's Companion* explores different perspectives on this topic. [4] The origin of its name is equally unclear. Andrew Kuntz suggests different possibilities, such as a reference to the German word "geige", which means violin. However, from Sonny Watson we learn that the word "jig" comes from the French word "gigue" and the Italian word "giga," which mean to jump or to dance.[5] In Italy, the giga was a dance with similar rhythmic characteristics as the Irish jig, both

---

[4] Andrew Kuntz, *The Fiddler's Companion - A Descriptive Index of North American, British Isles and Irish Music for the Folk Violin and other Instruments*, http://www.ibiblio.org/fiddlers/index.html, accessed October 23, 2006.

[5] Sonny Watson, *Street Swing.com, History of the Jig* - http://www.streetswing.com/histmain/z3jig.htm, accessed October 23, 2006.

having consecutive triplets. This is a plausible connection given that Irish harpers were known in Italy and the rest of Europe as early as the thirteenth century. The jig has always been referred to as a lively dance. It originated from an older dance form, the "Galliard" which had a similar upbeat spirit and was in triple time. If, indeed, the Irish did not invent this dance form, they adopted it and made it their own. The jig, with its immense popularity, therefore became known as the 'Irish' jig.

The jig was popular at the English court in the sixteenth century. According to Andrew Kuntz, Sir Henry Sydney wrote a letter to Queen Elizabeth in 1569, wherein the author enthusiastically reported the dancing of Irish jigs by Anglo-Irish ladies of Galway who, he said, were "very beautiful, magnificently dressed, and first-class dancers."[6] The gigue became a fashionable courtly dance at European courts during the Baroque era, including the court of Louis XIV. Musicians regularly played suites or sonatas at baroque courts, with dance movements incorporated into their compositions. Originally the gigue was added as a fourth movement in a suite after other dances such as the allemande, courante, and sarabande.[7] Later, the gigue was placed at the end of a suite, or as the last movement of a sonata. That final fast movement was called "Presto" or "Allegro" and had all characteristics of an actual gigue.

---

[6] Andrew Kuntz, *The Fiddler's Companion - A Descriptive Index of North American, British Isles and Irish Music for the Folk Violin and other Instruments*, http://www.ibiblio.org/fiddlers/index.html, accessed October 23, 2006

[7] Curt Sachs, *Geschiedenis der Muziek (Our Musical Heritage: A Short History of Music)*, Het Spectrum 1973, New York, NY: Prentice-Hall, Inc., 1955: 187, 188.

Gigue / Giga (last movement):

Johann Sebastian Bach
(1685-1750)

Partita III for solo violin, in E Major,
BWV 1006
Preludio - Loure - Gavotte en Rondeau - Menuet
I and II - Bourée - *Gigue* (in 6/8).

Johann Adam Birkenstock
(1687-1733)

Sonate in E Minor
Adagio - Corrente - Largo - *Giga* (in 6/8)

Arcangelo Corelli
(1653-1713)

Sonata VII for violin / b.c, in D Minor, op.5 # 7
Preludio - Corrente - Sarabanda - *Giga* (in 6/8)

Arcangelo Corelli
(1653-1713)

Sonata X for violin/b.c., in F Major, op. 5 # 10
Preludio - Allemanda - Gavotta - *Giga* (in 6/8)

Johann Joachim Quantz
(1697-1773)

Triosonate in E Minor
Adagio - Allegro - Affettuoso - *Giga* (in 6/8)

Gigue; Presto or Allegro (last movement):

Jean Baptiste Loeillet
(1680-1730)

Triosonate in G Major, op. 1 # 2
Grave - Allegro - Largo - *Allegro* (in 6/8)

Johann Christoph Pepusch
(1667-1752)

Triosonate in F Major
Largo - Allegro - Adagio - *Allegro* (in 6/8)

Johann Joachim Quantz
(1697-1773)

Triosonate in G Major
Andante - Allegro - Largo - *Presto* (in 6/8)

Baroque Performance Technique

When speaking of the right hand and the bow arm in his
book *Bach's Solo Violin Works*, Jaap Schröder writes:

*Well into the Baroque era, instruments of the violin
family were often held against the upper body at an angle
that caused the bow to move more vertically than hori-
zontally, with the right arm in a very low position. This*

bowing style, visible in many paintings and other works of art of the time, can still be observed with today's folk fiddlers and is in fact more natural – and certainly more relaxed – than the modern soloist's stance with a high elbow.[8]

Indeed, at the old-time jam sessions, I witnessed a number of similarities between baroque performance technique and old-time fiddling, most immediately in the areas of posture and bowing technique.

[8] Jaap Schröder, *Bach's Solo Violin Works - A Performer's Guide,* New Haven, CT: Yale University Press, 2007.

Posture, Bowing, Chin- and Shoulder Rest, Gravity

Holding violin in different positions: two Baroque holds (top row), and two fiddle holds (bottom row)

The way the violin is held for baroque performance is different from the modern violin hold. What currently is considered a good violin posture does not work well for a good and exciting rendition of baroque music. In order to get a relaxed feel, less emphasis is given to the violin being held 'high' on the shoulder. Without changing the position of the violin sitting on the shoulder, one can relax one's general posture. Originally, for dance music, the violin was held lower all together. Chin-rests weren't yet a part of the set-up of the instrument. Even today, some old-time fiddlers play the instrument without the chin-rest in a low position with the violin resting against one's breast and/or arm. This is quite similar to the early violin posture in the Renaissance and early Baroque eras.

During the Baroque era, violin technique differed based on the needs of the music. In those days the violin was built slightly different and did not have its current dimensions. Open strings were used as often as possible. Strings were made of gut and had a warmer, lighter sound, and the violinist would typically not play higher than in the third position.

In the late 1800s a shoulder-rest was invented to help support the hold of the instrument on the shoulder and increase the freedom of the use of the left arm and hand. No longer does the violinist need to help hold the instrument with the hand, thus giving the arm and hand complete independence for moving up and down the fingerboard. Fiddlers with some classical training are more likely to use a shoulder-rest. Not only does this improve the musician's posture, it gives more freedom to the left hand and allows for more virtuoso technique.

When I play baroque music I choose to use a shoulder-rest. I believe it supports my technique and total posture. I am less likely to raise my shoulder and warp my neck and thus create problems for my neck. I am less likely to tense up in my hand and arm, which might cause other health problems. And most importantly it gives me a great range of freedom to play the more virtuoso passages in baroque music, like in the Bach solo sonatas and partitas. For these reasons I always advocate using a shoulder-rest, no matter what musical style is played. I personally don't think it influences how we play any kind of music, whether it is old-time, bluegrass, jazz, classical or baroque.

Gravity plays a big role in baroque performance technique and is reflected in one's posture and way of playing. Try closing your eyes for a moment and breathing out and relaxing. You'll notice a feeling of a natural downward motion in your body. When sitting down in a similarly relaxed way, we can feel the weight of our body on the chair. This is a natural weight or the force of gravity. Musicians use this natural weight in bowing in baroque performance. The bow-arm leans somewhat down as it relaxes. This is not to be confused with a so called 'bad posture'. Just like the sensation of sitting on a chair, one can feel the arm relax and 'translate' a natural weight from the bow to the string. Jaap Schröder writes:

> *The bow is kept on the string by the weight of the arm; the first joint of the index finger acts as a kind of rudder and regulates the tone production. Modern playing technique contrasts starkly with this (the above) description: the arm and elbow are held parallel to or above the bowing line, and the sound is produced by pressure more than weight.*[9]

---

[9] Jaap Schröder, *Bach's Solo Violin Works–A Performer's Guide*, New Haven, CT: Yale University Press, 2007: 11.

A Circular Motion

An intense and strong sound can be produced using weight, mostly in the down-bow. The down-bow is a bow-stroke where the arm generally moves in a downward direction, along with a sense of gravity. The up-bow then will feel like breathing in, as the arm moves against gravity in an upward motion. This up-bow usually is a lighter bow-stroke that creates a circular movement. To practice this feel and bowing, initially the circular motion is exaggerated in the arm, causing the bow only to touch the string during the down bow. Ultimately, the bow doesn't leave the string and the up-bow will just sound slightly lighter. Jaap Schröder articulates the importance of this way of bowing when he writes:

> *The old bow, unlike the modern one, naturally dif-*
> *ferentiates between down- and up-bows, the up-bow*
> *being lighter in sound. It is the audible inequality of the*
> *baroque bow's movements, akin to the cadence of human*
> *breathing, that gives life to the music of the 18th c[en-*
> *tury]. Hence the all-important 'rule of the down-bow',*
> *which organizes the bow strokes according to the weight*
> *of the notes and their place in the bar.*[10]

It is this natural bow stroke that serves fiddlers very well and is one of the main reasons why some fiddlers like to use a baroque bow. Fiddlers advocate a similar bow action, based on this circular motion. Fiddlers at jam sessions and festivals tried to explain the circular motion of the bow to me as being a specific bow technique, unique to fiddling. Once I understood their explanations, it became clear to me that this very circular motion is not just the difference between baroque and modern violin

---

[10] Schröder, Ibid.: 16.

technique. It is also the difference between fiddle and modern violin technique.

Loose Wrist

Fiddlers profess the importance of the loose-wrist movement. Some of the finest fiddlers, such as bluegrass fiddler Byron Berline, have explained to me how different the bowing technique is, regarding the wrist movement. They emphasize that in order to play a well-sounding fiddle tune, it is imperative to have a loose wrist. It has come to their attention that violinists, on the whole, do not use that technique. To me this is a very interesting observation.

In order to use the circular bow-movement, which tends to be the norm among baroque violinists, one cannot ignore the wrist. The wrist in these strokes will have to be loose. The intense use of the lower part of the bow and the fast, crisp passages in baroque music invite a loose wrist. A typical sixteenth-note phrase with repeated string changes—as one can find for instance in music of Johann Sebastian Bach and Antonio Vivaldi—loses its character, intensity, and speed if it is executed exclusively with the arm. One can imagine a frantic arm-waving violinist, who may well be in trouble. Good violin technique involves the use of a loose wrist. However, the wrist is not the power source but rather the conductor of power driven by the arm. Violinists use the arm to support a full and varied sound. Therefore the use of the wrist is integrated in the total bowing technique of any good violinist. The use of the wrist is really dependent on the music itself and the style of music.[11]

---

[11] Louis Metz, *De Kunst van het Vioolonderwijs (The Art of Violin Education)*, part 2, Broekmans & van Poppel, 1965: 73-76.

Bows and Bow-Holds

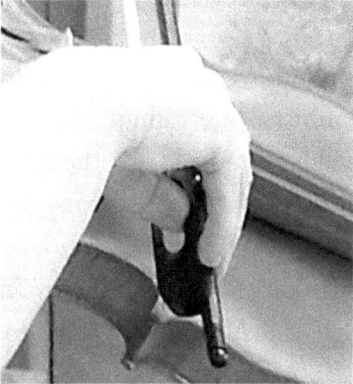

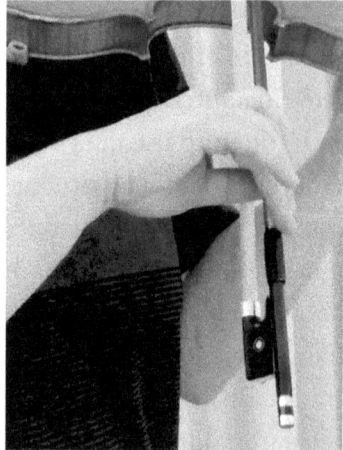

Bowholds (top row): fiddle bowhold higher up the bow and at the frog (thumb underneath the frog) and bottom row: Baroque hold at frog, and higher up the bow for lighter baroque feel (with modern bow).

Why do fiddlers hold the bow further up the bow and not right at the frog?

Baroque bows were built differently than the modern bow. In general, they were lighter, shorter and shaped differently. Baroque bows have become popular again, particularly since they support the bowing technique needed for baroque performance. The bow is shaped somewhat differently, too. Due to the different weight distribution a baroque bow is very versatile at the frog and lower half of the bow. This gives the violinist a chance to play fast runs crisply. However, playing with a baroque bow in a modern bow style and aiming for a sustained sound is more difficult. One is likely to run out of bow quickly and "crash" as well as struggle at the upper end of the bow. When holding the bow with a low arm position one can play a very slow bow stroke most beautifully with a lot of expression.

It is possible to play baroque music with a modern bow. The bow-hold is not necessarily different from the modern bow-hold. A violinist playing baroque music with a modern bow may well choose to place their right hand higher up the bow, away from the frog. This helps to create a lighter feel and approaches the feel of a baroque bow, facilitating bowing technique needed for baroque performance.

Among fiddlers it is not at all uncommon to pick up the bow similarly at a higher point, in order to get that lighter feel of the bow. Their needs are similar to the needs of the baroque violinist. Holding the bow at that higher point helps facilitate their needs.

Music Rhetoric

Music of the Baroque era (1600-1750) had its own particular style characteristics befitting the instrumentation of the period. Popular instruments include the harpsichord and other keyboards such as the spinet and virginal. The sound characteristics of these instruments were less versatile than the instrumentation of later periods, mostly due to technological limitations such as the plucking of strings in a harpsichord that did not offer sustained notes. Later keyboard instruments, like the piano, could be played with varying dynamics. The increased dynamic possibilities inspired composers like Mozart (1756-1791) and Beethoven (1770-1827) to explicitly indicate dynamic markings in their compositions. Baroque composers, on the whole, did not use dynamic markings. Music was written down and baroque musicians understand from the score how to play it. It is a very interesting phenomena to just look at sheet music and realize what tempo to take, what expression to give it, and what ornamentation to use. We are now in the field of rhetoric.

Modern copy of a Flemish eighteenth-century harpsichord
(image courtesy of Mikesch Muecke)

In the Renaissance period prior to the Baroque, music was used as an element of rhetoric, i.e. the persuasive, engaging and emotional aspect of a conversation and communication. This focus on rhetoric developed further in baroque music. Baroque musicians learned what ornamentation to use, even though it was not noted by the composer in the music.

The more you play baroque music, the more the music speaks to you. It is composed in a way that one can nearly hear the voice, the excitement, as a phrase intensifies, by a run going up in pitch or by a big leap in pitch. One can feel the relaxation as the phrase goes down in pitch. In short, the notes tell a story and the musician plays with this basic material using the guidelines of the time and culture. French, Italian and German baroque each have different ornamentations and interpretations, guiding the musician according to the musical culture of the time and their particular regional area or country.[12]

When exploring the rhetoric of baroque music it is intriguing to see how it compares with the different fiddle styles and fiddlers' set of expectations with respect to their musical performance. Fiddle music, too, has progressed in much the same manner as baroque music. Although traditionally fiddle music was not written but instead passed aurally from fiddler to fiddler, the similarity to baroque music in terms of individual interpretation is substantial. Much of the interpretation of fiddle tunes depends upon the cultural origin of the tune and on the fiddler's regional and cultural background. Even though a tune may be the same, fiddlers' interpretations are bound to be different, due to local traditions and possible influences from other fiddlers.

Today, many fiddle tunes are written down as sheet music. As in the baroque compositions, fiddle tunes are typically written in bare form without additional ornamentation. The experienced fiddler interprets, ornaments, and improvises the music according to the style of the tune and his or her musical background. This personal interpretation is how the tapestry of music interweaves with the local custom of playing.

---

[12] Elaine Thornburgh and Jack Logan, *Music in Our World; Baroque Music* http://trumpet.sdsu.edu/M151/logan_M151_MOW.html, accessed October 23, 2006.

Fiddle tunes that are written down are typically only one fiddler's interpretation of the tune within the style prevalent in their region. When traveling around the country, it is very likely one will hear a great diversity of interpretations of a particular tune. Fiddlers may choose to play different notes, single or double stops, different rhythms, and so on. On the whole, fiddlers will identify with a specific regional interpretation. The rhetoric of the tune thus belongs to the tradition of the region and the origin and roots of that region's particular fiddle style.

Old Joe Clark

Old Joe Clark is an example of a traditional fiddle tune played in many different ways. Originally *Old Joe Clark* was a ballad concerning an old mountaineer in Kentucky murdered for his shenanigans.[13] This popular old-time fiddle tune is embraced by bluegrass musicians who embellish it with many unwritten notes and a smoother bow-stroke, unlike old-time fiddlers who are more likely to play it with a "shuffle stroke" and added open string (a drone note). The tune, therefore, knows many renditions based on local traditions as well as outside influences. No matter the variations on the simple melody line, fiddlers tend to know

---

[13] See an all-star rendition: https://www.youtube.com/watch?v=QI7i7d4W2U4 Bluegrass twin fiddle, accessed May 4, 2015.
Fiddle John http://www.youtube.com/watch?v=DZw9hB1yNYY, accessed April 3 2015.
Casey Abair https://www.youtube.com/watch?v=0nDWVDkGuSs, accessed May 4, 2015.
Ole Rossell: https://www.youtube.com/watch?v=fCSKACeycT8, accessed May 4, 2015.
Michael: https://www.youtube.com/watch?v=BVw2NVQ3-L4, accessed May 4, 2015.

just how the tune is to be played. Indeed, the main tune, with its underlying chord progression, survives the rhetoric of all fiddlers. This is one example of many.

Rhythmic Aspects of Written Notation

Writing down a tune played by a fiddler is a challenge indeed, as the notation is unable to cover many subtle nuances heard in fiddle tunes. Articulation, phrasing, and the actual length of the notes vary and are often insufficiently reflected. Similarly, violin pieces are typically notated with a lack of precision regarding the exact intentions of the composer. Certain expressions as well as rhythmic interpretations cannot be adequately expressed on paper and it takes knowledge of the musical style to perform well what is written down.

'Notes Inégales' or Swing Strokes

In baroque music the French term *notes inégales* (*inégales* meaning 'uneven') is used as a guide for musicians to indicate that the rhythm is uneven although it is written otherwise—'straight'. For the fiddler, this is called a *swing stroke*. One may notice a clear difference between the printed version and the actual version performed by the fiddler. The printed version of a fiddle tune will typically display a straight rhythm of even or equal eighth notes. The experienced fiddler will lengthen the first of two eighth notes by just a tiny bit and create an uneven rhythm that is impossible to notate. This will be applied according to the feel and style of the tune.[14]

---

[14] In Irish fiddling an example of written notation as a guide and not an absolute is heard in the 6/8 notation. The three even notes usually are not performed with equal length. It takes practice to execute these fiddle

The rules, in support of the fashion and musical tastes of the time, culture, and country/region, were evidence of a sense of freedom in baroque performance interpretation. The fact that the term, *notes inégales* is French reflects its popularity among French baroque musicians. For example, with a slow tempo and conjunct melodic motion with a series of eighth notes, the first of each two eighth notes would be slightly elongated. This is not to be mistaken with the execution of a clear dotted rhythm. However, in some cases, the term applied to dotted or double-dotted notes. The French would say that taste determines where the unequal notes shall be a little or extremely dotted.[15] Anthoine Carre in his book about baroque guitar and tablature at the end of the seventeeth century writes, "Consider playing eighth notes inégales in this French baroque music. Let your ear be your guide."[16] Carre's idea of letting one's ear decide gives a sense of the freedom in interpretation to baroque musicians. How similar this is to the performance technique of different fiddle styles!

tunes in the Irish tradition. The more familiar one becomes with Irish fiddling, the more natural it will feel to perform fiddle tunes this way.

[15] Sol Babitz, *"Notes Inegales": A Communication," Journal of the American Musicological Society*, Vol. 20, No. 3, 1967: 473-476.

[16] Anthoine Carre, *Livre de Pieces de Guitarre et de Musique*, http://www.donaldsauter.com/antoine-carre.htm, accessed May 8, 2015.

Scordatura or Cross-Tuning

Although composers and performing musicians use musical terms in their own language in classical music Italian terms are commonly found. While a student in Amsterdam, I was introduced to the exciting phenomenon of *scordatura* (Italian for "*mis-tuning*"). *Scordatura* is an alternate tuning to help extend the range of the instrument, and make certain melodies and harmonies possible in passages and to create chords in particular keys. There are many tuning possibilities. For example, the tuning of the violin changes from the regular GDAE tuning to GgDd tuning, or to GDgb tuning which is a G Major chord. Also, the sound of the instrument changes. It rings differently and sounds especially rich in the chord in which it is tuned—a wonderful sensation for a musician!

Scordatura was used by European composers throughout the centuries for a variety of reasons. Wolfgang Amadeus Mozart (1756-1791) may have used it to make the viola sound louder by way of tuning the strings a semitone higher. Gustav Mahler (1860-1911) may have looked for a tone color or sound effect in his *4th Symphony*. A famous example of *scordatura* in the Romantic era can be found in *Dance Macabre* by Camille Saint-Saëns (1835-1921) where the solo violin tunes the E string down to an E flat.

The *Mystery Sonatas* by Heinrich Ignaz Franz von Biber (1644-1704) are a special *scordatura* feast. Each sonata is tuned in a different tuning, causing the violin to sing differently. When played, the tunings provide a totally new meaning as the ear hears a different set of overtones. The fingering can get very confusing since it is entirely possible to find yourself playing a lower note on what usually is a higher string, and so the notes on the strings literally cross due to this unconventional tuning.

In the world of fiddlers, *scordatura* is referred to as *cross-tuning*. It is used mostly in old-time fiddle tunes. Usually the strings are tuned to GDGD in the key of G, ADAE in the key of D, or AEAE in the Key of A. In these instances, fiddlers enrich the sound by adding a drone (a continuous note) on the open string next to the one on which the melody is played. Cajun fiddlers particularly like the aspect of the drone and use it a lot. Oftentimes to accommodate the key, fiddlers playing Cajun music will lower the pitch of all strings one step down to FCGD.

Having played the Biber sonatas, I have thoroughly enjoyed the rich sound and amazing possibilities on the instrument. Whether in baroque music or in fiddle music, the differently tuned strings offer an enriched sound experience.

Vibrato

Vibrato is a movement that causes a shake in the finger which results in a slight fluctuation in pitch. It enhances the resonance and richness of the sound. This added color may be used as ornamentation from time to time or it can be used more constantly. Fashion, taste and style of music are all elements that determine the use of vibrato. Vibrato in itself can vary substantially. Technically it can be executed in different ways. There is arm, hand and even finger vibrato. These different techniques facilitate a broad range of vibrato varying from narrow to wide, and from slow to fast depending on the versatility of the player. Ideally a violinist is able to apply the full scope of vibrato to accommodate the style of music he/she plays. A lack of technique can be the cause of an inability to adjust one's vibrato to the style of the music and may result in a constant 'un-controlled' vibrato. This way of playing might easily be perceived as being in bad taste.

The appropriate use of vibrato is a hot topic for fiddlers and violinists alike. Violinists are often accused of playing a constant and fast vibrato, whereas bluegrass fiddlers advocate a slower vibrato applied in slow passages, such as waltzes.

During the latter part of the twentieth century, baroque violin performance technique was reviewed and new ideas became popular. There was a strong belief that vibrato was not part of playing baroque music correctly. As time progressed, a realization grew among baroque musicians that playing fully without vibrato was a misconception. Vibrato, especially on longer notes, enhanced the music. It was paramount, however, not to use vibrato like a blanket to cover clarity of the notes and their expression. Vibrato could be used but only sparingly in baroque repertoire, as a coloration and ornamentation of particular phrases. Interestingly, non-vibrato in itself can also have an effect of color and ornamentation since it contrasts with vibrato on the other notes.

Among old-time fiddlers I have heard similar discussions and opinions being shared. Certain fiddlers are convinced that this particular style of fiddle playing must be without *any* form of vibrato while others, depending on their regional tradition, have a slightly varied idea allowing for limited use of vibrato. I vividly remember the comments of an old-time fiddle judge at a contest where some of the contestants were using vibrato while playing old-time tunes. It was his opinion that the use of vibrato was absolutely against the rules of old-time fiddling. However, another old-time fiddle judge, with a slightly different fiddle tradition, differed with that opinion and felt that some vibrato could be used, though sparingly.

This discussion makes me smile. I see reflected exactly the same issue among fiddlers that is alive among baroque musicians. How wonderful that the mystery of music keeps us that involved, and that music performance continues to progress unabated.

Chapter 3
The World of Fiddlers

Bluegrass jam session with Michael Peyton on banjo

L earning to play fiddle I have felt particularly challenged to know the chords that make up a fiddle tune. In fiddling, underlying chord progressions are the basis of the melody. A fiddler, specifically when wishing to improvise and play a "lead" or solo—a "break"—is required to know this harmonic structure. Even though scales[17] helped me understand a key, I would be completely lost trying to internalize chords quickly in the course of a jam session. For instance, I would know that D Major has two sharps, but not realize the structure of the chords[18] and what chords might be expected. I might easily play unrelated notes in a break, focusing on the melody. Things would go brilliantly for a while and folks were excited with my "break" (solo) and then all of a sudden there would be a clangor or discord or two, totally disturbing the flow of the music and throwing the other musicians off. I either hadn't played the notes that fit the chords we were playing, or progressed to a different key without knowing it and produced some very undesirable dissonant notes. I can't help but think I am not alone in that experience. No matter how well trained a classical musician, unless special attention was given within one's training, chord progression would pose a challenge when improvising.

Key and Chord Progressions

Fiddling demands the student to focus on the key and chord progressions, i.e., the harmonic structure. I believe it is very enriching for any musician to learn this vertical aspect while playing a melodic line. Music in general is a combination of linear and vertical movement. The melody and underlying harmony go hand in hand, and ignoring one of these takes away an

---

[17] Scale: A collection of pitches arranged in order from lowest to highest or from highest to lowest.

[18] Chord: three or more pitches sounded simultaneously; two such pitches are normally referred to as an interval.

essential element of music. Understanding both instantly while improvising, without first needing to access one's theoretical knowledge, seems an invaluable addition to one's versatility as a player and to one's musicianship.

The Aural Tradition

Another strong aspect of fiddling is the aural tradition. Whereas sheet music overall is currently an accepted tool for learning to play fiddle tunes, a traditional fiddler learns to play by listening and watching other fiddlers play. The process of learning aurally is not just learning a different way, but demands a much greater dependency on one's ears which strengthens one's musicianship. One is asked to be alert and assess all musical elements that together make up the tune such as key, rhythm, tempo, melodic line, harmonic structure, phrasing and special characteristics. [19]

Since fiddle tunes generally are not as complex as most of the classical repertoire, and since they tend to be repetitive with a simple binary form, e.g. AABB, fiddle tunes provide a great opportunity for the exploring violinist to experience a new way of learning and hearing music.

An immediate emphasis on analysis of the music is second nature to fiddlers. Typically in a jam session, one cannot just say, "Ah, I don't know this tune, let me go home and find a book

---

[19] Key: In tonal music, the pitch relationships that establish a single pitch class as a tonal center or tonic (key note), with respect to which the remaining pitches have subordinate functions. The key of a work is defined in terms of the particular major or minor scale from which its principal pitches are drawn.

that features this tune on sheet music. Let me then learn it and come back next week." In a jam session one has only an instant to absorb the tune and either play along or take a "break" (play a solo). Thus, immediate attention needs to be given to the key, chords, phrases, and peculiarities of the tune.

To experience fiddling is a great opportunity to learn to actively listen. It helps to prepare violinists for memorizing lengthy and involved violin pieces like concertos. It also helps create an adeptness to learn melodic and harmonic structure, even within the beginning stages of exploring that tune. This way the student pays close attention to the key, chords, expression, and musical line of the tune instead of merely playing the notes. The student develops a deeper understanding of the music, thus creating a habit of including awareness of harmony and other elements in the initial stages of learning a piece.

I have always been incredibly impressed with the tremendous musicianship presented by high level bluegrass musicians. Over time, I witnessed their impeccable skills in picking up the structure and melodic material of tunes unknown to them. In jam sessions it is a common courtesy to share the key and, if needed, some unusual chord progressions before playing the tune together. When it was time for the musicians to "get the break" they would be astonishingly accurate and creative in reproducing the tune and able to throw in some amazing variations, showing off their talent and virtuosity. At such moments I would feel the intense excitement of making music together, created "on the spot".

Byron Berline and George Custer (part of the Judges' Jam Session) on stage at the Sawgrass Fiddle Contest in Micanopy, Florida, 2006 (image courtesy of Humberto Herrera)

Judges' Jam Session onstage at the Sawgrass Fiddle Contest in Micanopy, Florida. Here are some of the finest musicians on stage together. From left to right: Jason Thomas, Tommy Slaughter, Jonathan Hodge, Byron Berline, George Custer, Alan Stowell, Mitch Corbin and Scott Anderson, 2006 (image courtesy of Humberto Herrera)

"Let The Tune Live Away From The Sheet!" - James Kelly

Is it wrong to learn from sheet music? Certainly not! When learning to play a tune, or musical piece of any kind, sheet music can be and is a great tool. This also holds true when learning fiddle tunes. However, it is not good to be glued to the sheet. I have seen many a violin student play a tune after they memorized it--with eyes fixed on an imaginary page. Whether the tune was played accurately or less so did not matter. Invariably the student would play the tune without real spirit or feel.

James Kelly and Annemieke Pronker-Coron at an Irish Fiddle workshop, led by James in Micanopy, Florida, 2004

Irish fiddler James Kelly reminded people at a workshop I attended in 2004 in Micanopy, "Do not depend on the sheet music. Use it as a tool and then learn to be the master of the tune. Let the tune live away from the sheet!" In other words, as you learn the tune, analyze it, and see what the notes mean. Where did they come from? Where do they go? What are the phrases? Then internalize the tune and make it your own. Play it many times and don't feel stuck with the exact instructions such as bowing and articulation on the page.

It is important to remember that fiddle tunes that are notated on sheet music are interpretations of one particular fiddler. As good as it is to absorb the instructions from the page and to learn the feel of the tune and its intentions, it is also important to leave the page behind and allow the tune to come alive in your own rendition.

What an incredibly wise lesson for a budding violinist! Even when keeping to the strict directions of the composer and sheet music, in order to play a piece well and let it come to life, it is a great notion to let the music "live away from the sheet."

In Their Own Words: What Four Famous Fiddlers Say About…

In my quest to learn more about fiddling and how to play fiddle I have had many conversations with a great array of fiddlers. I learned a lot from listening and watching them play, learning tunes and playing together in jam sessions, and hearing their stories. Listening to a fiddler explain what to do and how to play gave me a multitude of insights that varied from very specific to general discussions about "the feel" of playing fiddle. I would like to share some of the very meaningful tips and words of advice that I have learned over the years from four of my very favorite fiddlers. When I read these instructions and the advice as presented by all four fiddlers, I feel enriched. It is so exciting to hear what they share. Their expertise and experience is amazing and I treasure their workshops and master-classes. I hope you find this as inspiring as it was for me.

...Bluegrass Fiddling

Byron Berline (image courtesy of www.doublestop.com)

Byron Berline

Byron Berline is an incredible internationally known fiddler, smooth in his style and very exciting. He is a virtuoso fiddler of the highest order and my fiddle-hero. He played with a variety of fabulous bluegrass bands, including Bill Monroe and the Bluegrass Boys in 1966/67. Byron has played with famous musicians and stars, appeared in movies and toured the world, sharing his bluegrass music. He initiated and planned the Oklahoma International Bluegrass Festival that runs annually since 1997. Either in a private session or in a master class setting, I learned the following interesting tips, suggestions and advice.

Berline Tips

"It is imperative to have a loose wrist."
"Double stops and the knowledge of chords and chord progression lies at the base of bluegrass fiddling."
"Scales are a must."
"With bluegrass think of blues - real slurry: for traditional bluegrass - blues - that's what Bill Monroe told me… blues-grass."
Fiddle licks: *"A lick is a note-y rendition of a simple melody line."*
Circle bow strokes: "*For Texas type fiddling there is a counter clockwise motion with your wrist. Always start with a down stroke (pull)."*
How to learn tunes and make them your own: "*Create a bank of licks and double stops. Listen to recordings and study. Build up a repertoire by listening to other people and borrow ideas from their playing. Store a bank of licks in each key/chord and of double stops-they are a way to get into different chords and accommodate the different chord progressions."*
Bowing: "*Bowing depends on the tune. First, get the tune established in your head, either by hearing it played or through your own creativity. Then bow accordingly. The smoother the notes and melody, the higher up the*

bow you play. The more bite, the closer to the frog, such as when playing rhythm or a "kick off" at the beginning of a tune."

The shuffle: "*The shuffle versus double shuffle (Orange Blossom) or figure-eight bowing is important to master in order to achieve the fiddle sound. It is basic bowing. Mississippi Sawyer and Ragtime Annie are good examples of this bowing pattern."*

Chords: "*Learn all the double stops you know in a chord."*

General advice when learning tunes: "*First practice the tune the basic way and only then work on improvisation. Don't start off fancy."*

...Bluegrass Fiddling and Band Playing

Laurie Lewis and Fletcher Bright

In 1993 I went to a summer course in bluegrass fiddle at Elkins, West Virginia. There I was treated to a most wonderful learning experience with bluegrass fiddler and singer Laurie Lewis, and fiddler Fletcher Bright. During an intense week at the Augusta Heritage Center, Laurie and Fletcher took turns teaching us, a group of enthusiastic bluegrass fiddle fans. The following are some of their lessons.

Laurie Lewis

Like Berline, Laurie Lewis is an international bluegrass musician. Based in California she performs as a singer, song writer and fiddler with her own band, currently called Laurie Lewis and the Right Hands. She recorded many albums with original music. International Bluegrass Music Association executive director Dan Hays called Laurie "one of the preeminent bluegrass and Americana artists of our time. She spreads her talent over several genres—bluegrass, folk, country —and with the recognition she has within all those fields, I would certainly say she's one of the top five female artists of the last 30 years."

Laurie Lewis, 2011 (image courtesy of photographer Irene Young)

Lewis' Tips...

    About Playing Backup in A Band: *"You can play long bows behind a singer or another instrumentalist, or you can "chop" and then there are "fills"."*

    Fills*: "Fills are good to play when there are long held out areas or pauses between the melody lines or at the end of a verse."*

    Leaving Room: *"You don't have to play all the time. Do not fall in the pattern wherever there is a hole you've got to fill it. That doesn't leave room for anybody else to fill any holes."*

    Visual Contact: *"Visual contact helps a lot with knowing when to do what, because sometimes you can't really hear exactly what is happening."*

    Backup: *"You back up the verse or the chorus before your break. In a jam session it is like you give a signal: "Ok guys, I am going to take the next break - I am doing the primary back up here and I am the one that's going to take the next solo."*

Fletcher Bright (image courtesy of www.dismemberedtennesseans.com)

Fletcher Bright

Bright followed the fiddling of proto-bluegrass artists such as Arthur Smith and Tommy Magness, but he came under the spell—as did practically every fiddler of his generation—of Benny Martin and Chubby Wise, and this fusion of old-time fiddle tunes and bluegrass drive, speed, and intensity are hallmarks of his playing. His work as an instructor at summer music camps such as the Augusta Heritage Center (Elkins, West Virginia), Nash Camp (Cumberland Furnace, Tennessee), Bluegrass on the Beach (Portland, Oregon), Mark O'Connor's Fiddle Camp (Dickson, Tennessee), the Festival of American Fiddle Tunes

(Port Townsend, Washington), and Sore Fingers (Kingham Hill, England) has perhaps reached even wider audiences and has definitely directly touched more lives.[20]

Bright's Tips About Playing Fiddle

   About Lewis' 'Visual Contact' Fletcher adds: *"A lot of clutter if all play and it is not pretty!"*

   Backup: *" It is fun to come in very suddenly and at the very start maybe lay back. Back up can be quite a challenge."*

   Learn About the Style: *"Play along with a recording of a good fiddler or band. Play the lead or break (solo) and learn all the little details and little connections of the phrasing. This way you learn about the style."*

   Licks: *"Borrow licks and apply them in other tunes."*

   Loosen the Bow: *"Keep the bow hair looser, so the bow bounces less. Bluegrass and old-time fiddlers don't do a whole lot of bouncing, other than for instance with a "kick off" to a tune."*

   How to Start a Tune: *"Use a "lead in," "kick off," or "scratch in" lick. Benny Martin added a triplet to a scratch in lick. The first note of a tune is either a "one, three or five" (referring to the first, third or fifth step of a scale within a key, and belonging to the root chord of the key). If you are not going to scratch, a good way to start is to use a six-note lick. You have to be precise and punchy as you prepare the band for the tempo (beat), so use "saw*

---

[20] Fletcher Bright, *Fiddler Magazine* http://www.fiddle.com/Articles. page?Index=6&ArticleID=18032, accessed April 13, 2015.

strokes" (single strokes) versus slurs (more notes in one bow stroke). You can swing it and the band then will pick that up."

"Son of a Bitch I'm Tired:" "*They say Benny Martin originated this 'scratch in', playing a triplet and two eighth notes.*"

Loose hands: *"They talk about a 'loose left hand'. You got to have a 'loose right hand', too!"*

Long Bow Style: *"They talk about a "long bow-style." Arthur Smith (from Tennessee) was about the first fiddler who was tagged a "long bow" fiddler. All it really meant was they got away from the saw stroke. Anything away from the saw stroke is approaching a long bow. Get away from the standard shuffle and slur, however many notes you can. But keep the rhythm going."*

...Irish Fiddling

James Kelly (image courtesy of www.jameskellymusic.com)

James Kelly

"James Kelly, a native of Ireland, is one of the greatest Irish traditional fiddlers of our time. Born in Dublin, James grew up listening to and playing traditional Irish music."[21]

It was a tremendous pleasure meeting James Kelly in Florida. I heard him play at the Florida Folk Festival in White Springs on several occasions. I traveled to Miami where he showed me some bowing techniques, specific for Irish fiddling. I also enjoyed a couple of fiddle workshops taught by him. James Kelly was awarded a number of prestigious awards in the US and in Ireland, including the 2006 "TG4 Irish traditional musician of the year" award. James Kelly, a true gentleman and fun person to be around, is a great fiddle teacher, motivated to pass on his

---

[21] From his web site bio.

art to all willing to learn. When teaching his workshop he shared some simple, yet not to be overlooked aspects of learning to play a fiddle tune.

Kelly's Tips About Playing Fiddle and Learning to Play A Tune

"**Listen and study** *before you "do"."*

"Sing the tune."

"Find the key and play the scale."

"Look for patterns and then...Let the tune live away from the sheet!"

"In other words, as you learn the tune, analyze it, see what the notes mean. Where do they go, where did they come from, what are the phrases and so on. Then, internalize it and make the tune your own. Play it a lot and don't feel stuck with the exact instructions on the page such as bowing and articulation."

Chapter 4
Building Bridges: Connections Between Baroque, Classical-Romantic, and Fiddling Performance Practice

My approach to playing a sonata by Johannes Brahms (1833-1897) composed during the Romantic era is very different from playing a sonata by Johann Sebastian Bach (1685-1750) composed during the Baroque era. Playing music from the Romantic Era requires a warm sound, filled with vibrato and the ability to play intensely connected sound utilizing a very well-defined bow technique. I do enjoy playing Brahms' sonatas and other music from the nineteenth century. However I also enjoy playing baroque music that requires a much lighter approach, with clarity and rhythmic precision. The music of J.S.Bach would be smothered were I to use the technique and approach required by Brahms, just as music by Brahms would lack richness were I to reverse the approach and apply my baroque technique to romantic repertoire.

Violin Performance Technique

Performance technique refers to how we play an instrument to support the style of music we perform. Goals of performance technique are to enhance the music and its intended expression. No matter what style of music we play, if our basic technical command of the instrument is not good, the music will not sound good. If we have difficulty playing in tune, music will not sound right. This is the most elementary way of looking at performance technique.

Basic technique on the violin required for mastery includes the following elements:

Good posture *facilitates the ability to pull a bow on the strings and allows the left hand to place the fingers, without squeezing or having to tightly hold the neck of the instrument.*

Produce a good sound *with the ability to get louder and softer.*

Listen actively.

Play in tune *by placing and lifting fingers accurately (finger action).*

Be able to articulate *a series of notes in different ways, such as legato (connected) or detaché (separated).*

Play rhythmically.

Play higher up the string *in positions which gives variety to tone color (timbre) and allows for a larger pitch range.*

Vibrato: Apply vibrato *by a shaking motion of the fingers to create a warmer, richer sound.*

Beyond this basic level, the next step is to apply the acquired technique to perform in a musical way. One can choose to play a piece of music in different ways with different fingerings (fingers and finger combinations we use for playing certain notes), bowings, and articulations. For example, in first position one can choose to play a note with the little finger or with a simple open string. Technically, the open string appears easier. However, what is more musical? If one is comfortable with using the little finger, the choice to cover the string will produce a warmer sound. However, it might be that a clearer sound (open string) works better to express the music at hand.

One can choose to play several notes in one bow stroke in a fast passage, or play all notes with separate bow strokes. Slurring the notes in one bow stroke may cause for a less hectic yet also less pronounced articulation. From another point of view, separate bow strokes may be more exact, yet slow the player down as technically it may require a higher level of proficiency. If the basic technique is well mastered, the musical expression required for a particular passage will lead to the final choice.

Not only particular pieces or passages but different styles of music require different uses of technique. One style of music may sound clearer and livelier with little or no vibrato. Another may flow better with a lot of intense and warm (wider) vibrato and yet another style may require narrow, more measured vibrato.

Development of Technique and Musicality

Typically when a student first learns to play the violin, the main focus is on a number of aspects varying from how to hold the instrument physically to intricate details of music interpretation, including dynamics, musical phrasing and articulation. A violin teacher most likely will focus on basic elements of technique such as posture, bowing, left and right hand coordination, sound and intonation.

Good Posture, Bow-Hold and Left-Hand Hold

How we stand or sit and how we hold the violin is important to prevent possible tension-related injuries so we can play more effectively and accurately. The violin appears not to be situated naturally in relation to our body, yet we can learn to create a natural hold. An awkward hold will make playing much harder and may cause some real physical damage as it will induce stress on certain muscle groups. When held correctly and tension free, the violin can be played with great precision and variety in expression.

Good Technique for Accuracy in Bowing, Intonation,[22] and Timing Coordination

A good bow technique facilitates versatile sound production, leaving room for great variety and musical expression. Clearly, if a violinist plays in tune, it is more pleasing to the ear than an out-of-tune sound. When we first start learning to play the violin, we easily stumble on the timing between the left hand and the bow. If this timing is not coordinated, we will hear a note that is bowed but doesn't change correctly to another note. Hence, coordination and accurate finger-action are basic

[22] Intonation: The degree to which pitch is accurately produced in performance.

techniques to accommodate good violin technique. Once basic technique is developed, the focus can expand to more advanced and specialized technique.

Technique to Facilitate the Ability to Play Sonatas, Concertos and Virtuoso Pieces

More advanced pieces require an array of more complex techniques for both the bow and the left hand. The left hand reach of notes is no longer confined to first position. Scales are played in two or three octaves. More notes are played simultaneously, such as double stops or chords. Trills are added, as well as a great variety of bow strokes such as martelé, spiccato, or legato.[23]

Rubato Versus Strict Timing

Tempi and rhythm are taught yet it is not unlike classical music to allow for some rubato[24]. The budding violinist may grow accustomed to some rhythmic freedom in the area of timing. To stretch the pulse a little to accommodate a difficult passage is not unheard of, whereas I believe this to be significantly more problematic in fiddling where the beat or pulse drives the music.

---

[23] Martelé: [French] "Hammered" bow-stroke. (APC) / Spiccato [It., strong; marked] bouncing the bow on the strings. (APC) / Legato [It., bound] smooth and connected bow-stroke. (APC)

[24] Rubato: [It. tempo rubato, stolen time]. In performance, the practice of altering the relationship among written note-values and making the established pulse flexible by accelerating and slowing down the tempo.

Vibrato and Sound Projection

In preparation for the popular virtuoso romantic pieces, a lot of emphasis is given to vibrato[25] and sound projection. Music historian Curt Sachs explains that "one of the most remarkable traits of that time (1760-1910) was the increasing interest of the musicians for the number of performers and for sound intensity." He goes on to say that

> *for the period between 1760 and 1910 the sole charac-teristic desire was to make the often playful and always moderate mental state so far, a desire to come to the extremes of expression: to achieve an almost inaudible pianissimo in the most esoteric chamber music or noisy, overwhelming fortissimos in orchestral music.* "[26]

Going More Deeply into Interpretation of Various Musical Styles

At this point one enters the field of interpretation, a fascinating topic when playing any music. In the course of history, musicians have argued about how to interpret compositions and the musical style or era they represent. How does one play Mozart or Beethoven? Both represent the Classical era. How do we play music from the Romantic era? When do we use slides? How do

---

[25] Vibrato: [It., from Lat. vibrare, to shake]. A slight fluctuation of pitch used by performers to enrich or intensify the sound. In modern string playing, vibrato is produced by rocking the left hand, usually from the wrist, as a note is played.

[26] Curt Sachs, *Our Musical Heritage, a Short History of Music*, New York, NY: Prentice Hall, Inc,, 1973, 6th print.

we execute trills? Do we start a trill with the note above, or with the note itself? How one interprets music of the different eras depends greatly on the musical fashion of the time and country. For instance, in the Romantic era it was the musical fashion to play music with vibrato and sustained sound, expanding the musical line as long as possible. During the nineteenth century this way of playing was applied to all music, including baroque music that had been composed earlier in Europe during the seventeenth and eighteenth centuries.

Changes in interpretation and performance technique were also closely connected to the metamorphosis of the actual instrument, from a baroque violin to a modern instrument, among other musical and technical changes that influenced the different music time periods that followed the Baroque era.

Intertwining Action and Re-Action among Violin Builders, Composers and Performers

It is interesting to explore how different aspects connected to the performance of music intertwined with and reacted to each other. The rise of the middle class and move to focus large musical performances away from courts and into public concert halls, and the development of chamber music brought into homes of the more wealthy as well as of the middle class, changed music composition and performance. With these changes came new instrument designs.

Originally baroque music was played on instruments created in the sixteenth and seventeenth centuries. The first violins (with four strings, tuned in fifths) were listed and illustrated around 1550, and the first violins were probably built by lute builders. It is likely that the northern Italian town of Brescia had the first violin makers within its gates.[27] The instruments were built differently than the violins we are familiar with today. They produced a smaller, more intimate sound, matching other period instruments such as the harpsichord, recorder and viola da gamba.[28]

Front views of Baroque violin, left, and modern violin, right
(images courtesy of Basil de Visser)

---

[27] Louis Metz, *Strijkinstrumenten Vroeger en Nu (String instruments Then and Now)*, Broekmans & van Poppel, 1974: 38.
[28] Viola da gamba: an instrument belonging to the viol family, held between the legs. A forerunner of the cello.

The differences between baroque and modern violins revolve around tension. A baroque violin was built with less tension on the instrument. The neck was shorter and was situated straight in relation to the body of the instrument. Nowadays the neck sits at an angle in relation to the body. The lighter baroque fingerboard sat on a wedge on the neck. Baroque strings were of a lower tension made of gut versus the modern synthetic and steel-wound strings. The strings were tuned at a lower pitch (A = 415 Hz[29] or even lower) than the pitch we commonly recognize today as an A (=440 Hz). In general violins were constructed lighter and had a lighter bass-bar.[30]

Baroque bows, too, were built differently, but worked well in response to baroque music. The bows were versatile and lightweight, giving the player an opportunity to articulate in the fashion of the time, i.e. accentuating down-bows and playing lighter up-bows.[31] There were many different bow designs and little uniformity.

Although the features of the baroque bow were not consistent from bow to bow, the lighter baroque bow is distinguished from the modern bow. A variety of woods was used for the baroque bow, such as snake wood, versus the pernambuco that is used for modern bows, or even fiberglass bows that became popular in the late twentieth century. The bows originally curved outward (convex). They were shorter, around 3/4ths of the length of a

---

[29] 415 Hz: the frequency in the International System of Units (SI). It reflects the standard frequency for the pitch (A2 – above the middle C).

[30] Metz, *Strijkinstrumenten Toen en Nu (String instruments Then and Now)*, Broekmans & van Poppel, 1974: 43.

[31] Down-bow / Up-bow   During the down-bow the hand moves away from the violin; during the up-bow the hand moves toward the violin.

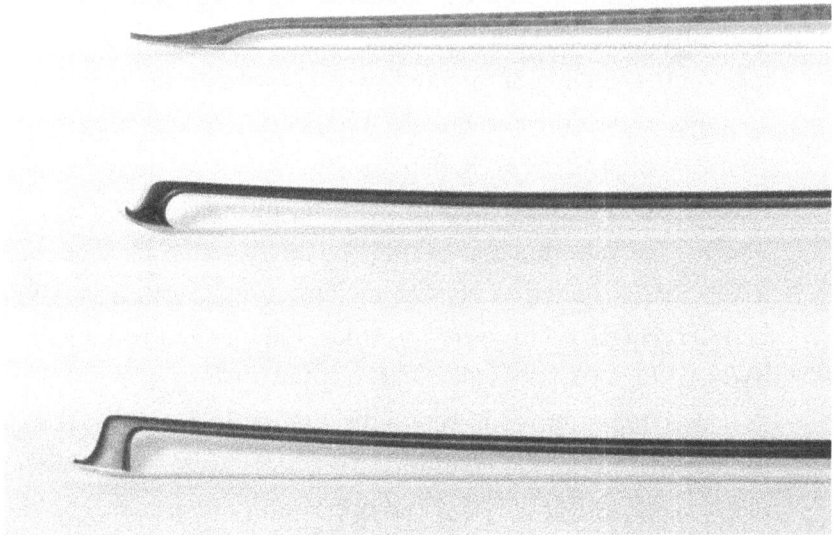

modern bow. Baroque bows had a different weight distribution than the later bows. They had less hair and less overall tension. Typically the bow would have a fixed frog. This changed with the later classical bow that featured a screw mechanism to tighten and loosen the hair. An interesting note is the use in modern bows of the *ferrule*, the nickel-silver part that holds the bow hair to the frog. The ferrule causes the bow hair to come together like a ribbon. This ribbon or hair bundle allows a more powerful approach, and makes strokes such as staccato and martelé possible. The baroque bow does not have a ferrule and the hair is more loosely spread. Instant accents are not possible. "The use of the martelé bow stroke in early music shows ignorance of this fact."[32]

---

[32] Metz, *Strijkinstrumenten Toen en Nu (String Instruments Then and Now)*, Broekmans & van Poppel, 1974.: 151.

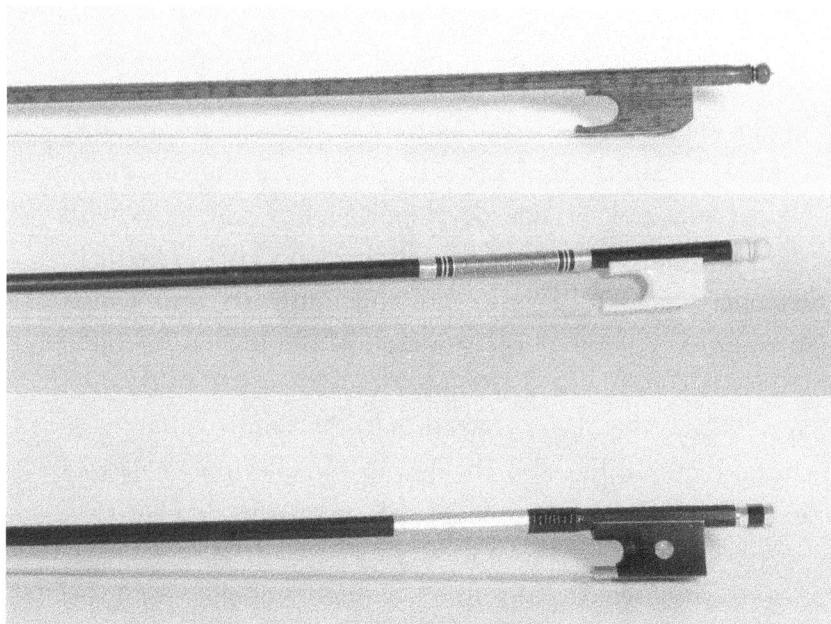

From top to bottom: baroque bow, classical bow and modern bow
(images courtesy of Basil de Visser at www.baroquebows.com)

The effect of the lighter and less tense bow was that the bow was perfectly suited for quick short strokes. It was accommodating a crisper articulation and a great agility. "The old bow, unlike the modern one, naturally differentiates between down – and up-bows, the up-bow being lighter in sound. It is the audible inequality of the baroque bow's movements, akin to the cadence of human breathing, that gives life to the music of the eighteenth century."[33] However, the bow would not allow for a sustained sound and would naturally decrease in sound when bowed from the frog to the point (down bow). The later

---

[33] Jaap Schröder, *Bach's Solo Violin Works–a Performer's Guide*, New Haven, CT: Yale University Press, 2007: 16.

design for the transitional classical bow helped the violinist to sustain sound more evenly. As time progressed and concert halls were built, emphasis was given to a bigger sound. Violin and bow makers developed violins and bows with this in mind. During the Classical period (1750-1820) in Europe, the middle class arose and music enjoyed a high status within their social structure. Music moved from the courts to living rooms (chamber music) in private homes, as well as to the bigger concert halls. Not only was a bigger sound required but also changes to the instrument needed to be made to accommodate the increasing emphasis on virtuosity. Therefore violins were designed with a longer fingerboard to assist the need to play in higher positions (higher up the fingerboard). Instrument builders adjusted the angle of the neck and lengthened the bass bar to create a higher tension while the pitch moved up to A = 430 Hz. Over time the tension as well as the pitch of the instrument has gradually increased, now surpassing A = 440 Hz. This is particularly the case in the vast concert halls where a louder and more brilliant sound seems paramount.[34]

The modern bow is based on the model of bows made by French bow-maker François Tourte (1747-1835). Tourte developed a newer bow model in France in the 1780s using pernambuco wood. This wood that was imported into France for making textile dye was chosen for its strength, beauty and weight. The pernambuco bow was less dense and stiff than the

[34] Filip Kuijken, *Construction and Repair of violins – violas – cellos / Baroque, Classic and Modern*: http://www.kuijkenviolins.com/baclamo/, accessed May 5, 2015.

earlier snake wood bows. This modern bow, with the changes as described above, encouraged a different bowing technique. It enabled musicians to draw out strong sustained notes and make interrupted bow strokes, e.g., staccato and martelé.[35] With the help of Italian violin virtuoso Giovanni B. Viotti (1755-1824), Francois Tourte developed his famous design of the modern bow. Here is an example of the interaction between a music performer and instrument builder to design, in this case, the modern bow.

The changes that were made in both the violin as well as the bow design allowed for an overall larger sound. They responded to the requirements for successful performance in large concert halls. The modern bow allowed for a more sustained sound, and the modern violin was built with a higher tension. Composers such as Felix Mendelssohn and Johannes Brahms were influenced by the newfound versatility of the instrument. The interaction took place between the instrument builders, performers, composers, and acoustics of performance environments.

In the Classical era a new emphasis on dynamics came along with the birth of the fortepiano, the successor to the harpsichord. New dynamic subtleties such as crescendo and decrescendo were feasible on the recently invented piano, and composers enjoyed new musical possibilities.

Performance technique changed considerably. The violin lent itself beautifully to the increasing range of dynamics now required by the compositions. The bow answered to a different

[35] Gabrieli Consort & Players, *The Monteverdi Violins*, www. themonteverdiviolins.org/baroque-violin.html, accessed May 5, 2015 and Jaap Schröder, *Bach's Solo Violin Works—a Performer's Guide*, New Haven, CT: Yale University Press, 2007: 13- 16.

and expanded world of articulation and the fingerboard allowed for a greater use of positions, varying sound-color by way of playing higher up the strings. A warmer sound was sought and found, answering to the musical taste in the Romantic era (1820 - 1900). Playing high up the strings not only helped create this sound but also expanded the pitch range of the instrument.

Musicians similarly explored vibrato. The use of vibrato evolved from a momentary effect or ornamentation. Its use went from sporadic and light use in the Baroque era to more common use and even continuous vibrato in the twentieth century. There is quite a bit of dispute regarding the historical use of vibrato.[36]

---

[36] Frederic Neumann, *The Vibrato Controversy*, Performance Practice Review, Claremont http://scholarship.claremont.edu/cgi/viewcontent. cgi?article=1058&context=ppr, accessed May 6, 2015. Frederick K. Gable, *Some Observations concerning baroque and Modern Vibrato*, Performance Practice Review, Claremont http://scholarship.claremont.edu/cgi/ viewcontent.cgi?article=1105&context=ppr), accessed May 6, 2015.

Niccolo Paganini (1782–1840). Source: http://en.wikipedia.org/wiki/
Niccolò_Paganini#/media/File:NiccoloPaganini.jpeg, accessed 23 May, 2015

Performers exploited the possibilities of new instruments, particularly during show pieces or cadenzas of concertos. Virtuoso violinists like the legendary Niccolo Paganini (1782-1840) inspired composers including Frédéric Chopin (1810-1849) and Robert Schumann (1810-1856). A wonderful connection of intertwining action and reaction within the music development can be witnessed. Virtuoso violinists also composed such as Niccolo Paganini, Fritz Kreisler and Eugène Ysaÿe (1858-1931).

Interpretation of Baroque Music
in the Romantic Era

As musical style changed in the Baroque to the Classical and then to Romantic eras, so did the *interpretation* of baroque music. In the nineteenth century the new instruments and performance techniques were applied to the interpretation of earlier baroque music.

Full sound and large bow strokes became part of the baroque interpretation of the more romantic fashion. Continuous vibrato and even slides were deemed appropriate. Tempi were interpreted differently. An example of this is by counting a slow movement in six beats per measure instead of the baroque intended two pulses. In this way, the melody was stretched to give a feeling of suspense, which was a very romantic notion. The natural line as provided by the baroque composition was lost in the emphasis on playing all smaller notes that lay in between two big pulses or pillars. To illustrate this difference,let us compare and contrast two different performances of the second movement "Largo ma non tanto"of the *Concerto for Two violins in D Minor, BWV 1043* by J.S. Bach (1685-1750). A performance by Jaap Schröder and Christopher Hirons with the Academy of Ancient Music sounds remarkably different from a performance by Yehudi Menuhin and David Oistrakh.[37] All four violinists are incredible musicians. However, while the first pair emphasizes the two pulses or pillars quite clearly, the other pair excels in continuous vibrato and sustained sound with a great emphasis on all smaller notes. Here are two very different interpretations of the same composition.

Yehudi Menuhin and David Oistrakh. Sources: http://en.wikipedia.org/ wiki/David_Oistrakh#/media/File:David_Oistrakh_1972.jpg and http:// upload.wikimedia.org/wikipedia/commons/a/a1/Yehudi_Menuhin_%26_ Stephane_Grappelli_Allan_Warren.jpg, both accessed May 23, 2015.

[37] DVD: *Oistrakh, Menuhin, Rostropovitch* , EMI video 90450 - Classic Archive 2003.
CD: *In Memoriam: Yehudi Menuhin,* Music & Arts 1053.
CD: *Johann Sebastian Bach: Violin Concertos Nos. 1 & 2 / Concerto for 2 Violins - The Academy of Ancient Music / Christopher Hogwood - Jaap Schröder and Christopher Hirons, violin,* Decca / Éditions de L'oiseau-Lyre B000004CX4 1990.

These romanticized interpretations continued into the latter half of the twentieth century and are still practiced nowadays. In the 1960s baroque music and its interpretation received much attention in Europe. In the late 1950s American violinist Sol Babitz (1911-1982) aggressively promoted a 'correct' historically informed way of playing the baroque violin.[38] New research led to musicians starting to use instruments built to the original baroque specifications. The use of gut strings and baroque bows became popular again. I witnessed how Amsterdam became a hub of activity in this specialization. Baroque ensembles formed, introducing interpretations of baroque music that were new to the listener. Slow movements were performed at faster tempi, revealing a pulse unfamiliar to the public more accustomed to a more romantic interpretation. Other performance aspects were treated similarly. Musicians used vibrato sparingly, if at all. Bowing focused on shorter and lighter strokes, creating air in phrasing. Ornamentations were intensely discussed and applied, including free improvised passages. Nikolaus Harnoncourt (b.1929), Austrian conductor as well as cellist and viola da gamba player, was a leader in this movement to more authentic performances of baroque music.[39]

After an initial transition time, this new twentieth-century school of baroque performance technique caught on and thrived in Europe, with Basel, London and Amsterdam as some of the major centers. As part of my studies with Jaap Schröder I was also

---

[38] Schröder, *Bach's Solo Violin Works*, New Haven, CT: Yale University Press, 2007: 3.

[39] Nikolaus Harnoncourt, *Baroque Music Today: Music As Speech: Ways to a New Understanding of Music*, Portland, Oregon: Amadeus Press, 1995.

fortunate to participate in a special workshop, Arcadia/Rhetoric in Music, led by Jos van Immerseel (fortepiano and harpsichord specialist) and Jaap Schröder. From both I learned a great deal about baroque performance technique.

Concertgebouw, Amsterdam (image courtesy of Claire Bontje and Hans Samsom)

Unlike the Baroque period (1600-1750) when sonatas, suites and other pieces for small ensembles were the main offered repertoire, during the Classical (1750-1820) and Romantic (1820-1910) eras concertos and symphonies for gradually expanding orchestras became more common. Big concert halls could accommodate larger audiences. Musicians were expected to be able to "fill the hall" acoustically by using vibrato as well as good bow technique.

Likewise fiddlers adjusted their techniques based on circumstances and popularity of the music. Both old-time fiddling and the baroque way of playing violin used little vibrato, small bow strokes and a more relaxed sound.. Microphones and amplification of the acoustic instruments made it possible for fiddlers to stay focused on a more relaxed bowing technique.

By the mid twentieth century, Bill Monroe and The Bluegrass Boys introduced "a new hard-edged style of country that emphasized instrumental virtuosity, close vocal harmonies, and a fast, driving tempo."[40] Vibrato, longer bow strokes and other techniques were introduced to accommodate the more virtuoso approach. Bluegrass bands performed in larger halls such as the Grand Ole Opry.

Ralph Stanley and the Clinch Mountain Boys at Edale Bluegrass Festival, Edale, England, 1991 (image courtesy of Annemieke Pronker-Coron)

[40] Stephen Thomas and Rovi Erlewine, *online biography of Bill Monroe*, http://www.billboard.com/artist/6206950/bill-monroe/biography, accessed April 10, 2015.

Cadenzas - Improvised in Baroque Music; Composed in Classical, Romantic, and 20th century Violin Concertos

During the Baroque era improvisation had a prominent place. Musicians were expected to fill in longer notes with ornamentation, drawing from a collection of ornaments including trills and short phrases. *Cadenzas*—virtuoso solos inserted into a movement in a concerto or other work, usually towards the end of the piece—demonstrated the musician's creative and technical abilities. Baroque compositions typically left a fair bit of room for the creation of cadenzas by just indicating a long note.

Baroque example of a violin sonata by Elisabeth–Claude Jacquet de la Guerre (1665-1729)

It was expected that the soloist would improvise a solo passage within the parameters and atmosphere of the piece.

During the Classical and Romantic eras cadenzas of violin concertos no longer were freely improvised. Although some virtuoso violinists still created their own cadenzas, usually they were written by the composer or a prominent violinist, and have become a supplemental part to the composition. An example of a famous composed nineteenth-century cadenza is in the Violin Concerto in E Minor, Op. 64 by German composer Felix Mendelssohn (1809-1847).

19th-century example of a composed cadenza for the first movement of the Violin Concerto by Felix Mendelssohn in E Minor, Op. 64

An example of a composed cadenza in the twentieth century is by Friedrich "Fritz" Kreisler (1875-1962), a prominent Austrian violinist and composer who wrote cadenzas, such as the one for the first movement of the Violin Concerto in D Major, Op. 61 by Ludwig van Beethoven (1770-1827).

*Cadenza composed by Fritz Kreisler for the first movement of the
Violin Concerto by Ludwig van Beethoven in D Major, Op. 61*

Interpreting the Composed Piece: Melody Line and Harmonic Structure

When we speak of the violin as a melody instrument, does that mean violinists need not focus on the underlying harmonic structure? Classical music for violin tends to be composed with a great deal of precision and intricacy. This requires the violinist to focus on the interpretation of the melody line to a level of perfection. Interpretation therefore receives much attention in the teaching practice, including articulation, phrasing, dynamics, and tempi.[41] These are all classical music performance elements that are a priority to the violinist. It is interesting to note that violinists may have difficulty relating the melody to the underlying harmonic structure of the composition.[42] The melody line is visible, ready to be played. If one focuses on the melodic line, one may not see the relationship with the harmony. The more experienced violinist, however, realizes that it is the harmonic structure that is the basis of the melody and helps determine the expression of that particular melodic line. Of course it is possible to intuitively play the melody with a general sense of harmony. It is important, though, to realize the difference between intuition and analyzing the key and chord progressions. It is this knowledge that deepens the music interpretation of the performer.

---

[41] Articulation: In performance, the characteristics of attack and decay of single tones and the means by which these characteristics are produced
[42] Harmony: [fr. Gr., Lat. harmonia]. The relationship of tones considered as they sound simultaneously, and the way such relationships are organized in time. / Harmonic structure (of the phrase) The phrase is the basic unit in which tonality may be established, projected, or changed by means of harmony. A phrase has harmonic structure as much as melodic or rhythmic structure.

In my experience, harmony was taught as part of music theory education rather than being integrated into violin performance lessons. Although I recall one of my violin teachers working on this aspect, on the whole I feel it is put on the backburner. Learning harmony, chord progressions and key relationships separately from playing the violin causes one not to relate to these easily. Often one can go a long way just sensing chord progressions and having a general understanding of the composer's intentions and musical form in which the piece was written, e.g. sonata or rondo. A violinist may be able to explain verbally where tension in a melody finds its high point and where it relaxes, and be able to interpret how to play that melodic phrase. Interestingly the tension and relaxation in a musical phrase is mainly created by chord progressions of the underlying harmonies. It takes extra effort to relate the visible melody to the harmonic structure. It is my experience that it is very enriching to incorporate the knowledge of the chord structure in one's performance. It is like adding a third dimension to a painting.

Coming Full Circle

My impression from learning more about fiddle music and its development into different styles is, contrary to what fiddlers and violinists say, that fiddling and violin techniques enhance each other and do not need to interfere with each other. They have close kinship as they developed from some similar roots like the dance music of the seventeenth century in Europe.

At the conservatory in Amsterdam I learned a great deal about baroque performance technique. Later, on my fiddle journey, I started to recognize some of the same techniques being utilized in the fiddle field. To me, it felt somewhat like coming home and completing the circle—one circle in a fabulous tapestry made up of circles that intertwine and represent music in all its many forms and glory.

Throughout my life I have translated and explained the various aspects of life by painting pictures of circles in my mind—circles that overlap with other circles. I experience my journey in music as being on a road that doesn't just lead from point A to point B. My musical journey has led to new areas that I had not experienced and yet that were based on the very technique I had learned in my musical hometown of Amsterdam.

Tom Staley, Fay Baird, and Michael Kemp playing old-time music together in Gainesville, Florida, 2015 (image courtesy of Mikesch Muecke)

Mountain music from the Appalachians was passed on via an aural tradition, since sheet music was not part of this musical heritage. The technique of playing was passed on this way, too. And like a language that evolves away from its roots, typically some of the older words and phrases are still used in the 'breakaway' language. In this case, the breakaway language is old-time fiddling and the original language of early violin playing in the Renaissance and Baroque eras in Europe.

As a Dutch native I recognize that certain words and phrases in Afrikaans, the language spoken in South Africa, are Dutch, yet never used by me. I am able to understand them by deduction and then realize that these words were part of the language of the Boers, Dutch people who emigrated to South Africa centuries ago. The Dutch language evolved and changed these original words and phrases to a modern Dutch version. Afrikaans, the breakaway language, filled with old Dutch phrases, appears to have undergone a similar evolution as old-time music has. Both were carried by a migrant population. The roots of both modern Dutch and Afrikaans are found in Europe. The roots of both old-time fiddle music and classical violin music are found in Europe. Baroque violin music and its performance technique bear witness. By visiting old-time jam sessions, I recognized that fiddle music originated in Europe during the Renaissance and Baroque eras.

The following is a Venn diagram illustrating the ideas of overlapping circles and influences as music is an inherent part of the world's history. This is an incomplete diagram showing

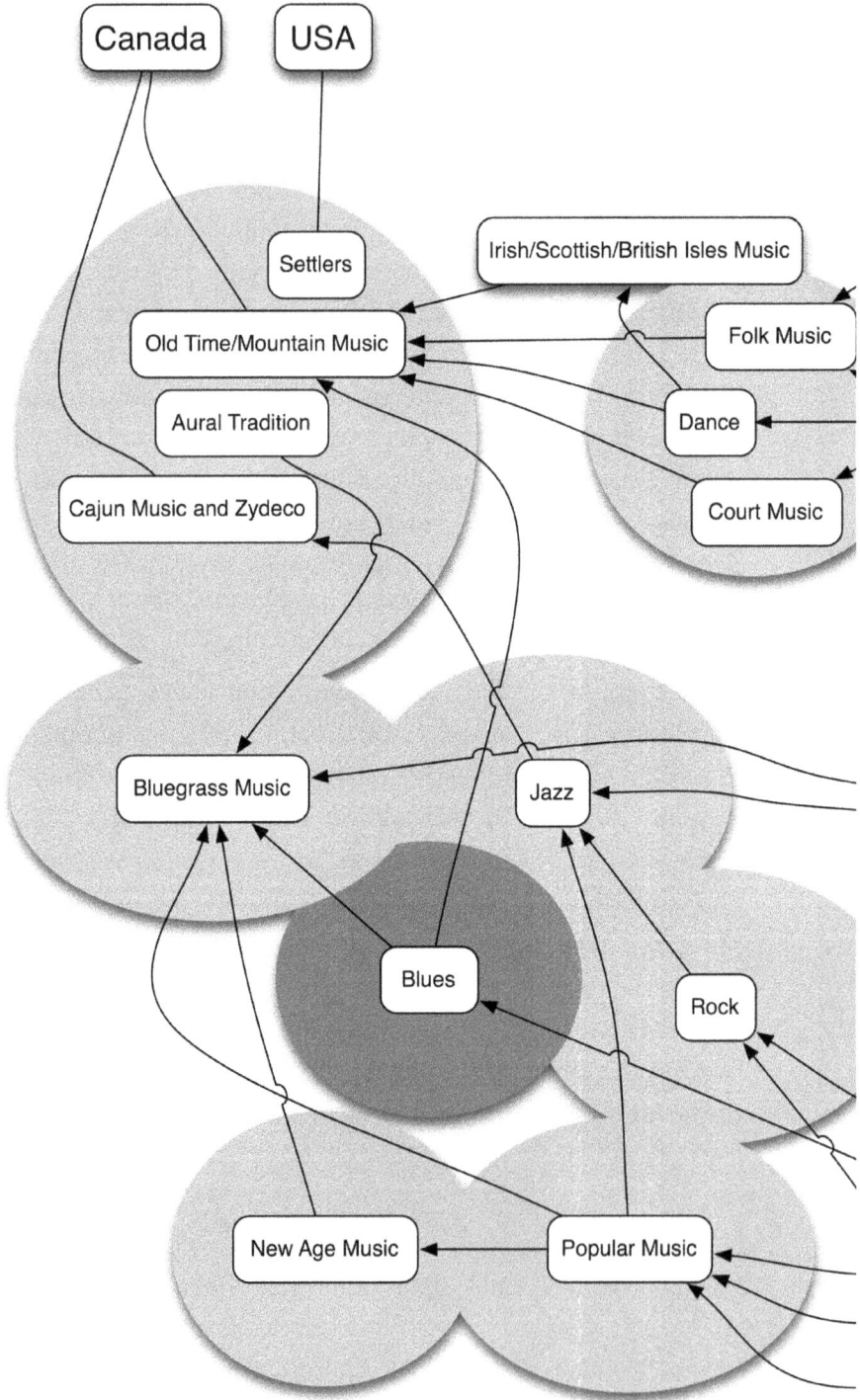

Canada

USA

Settlers

Irish/Scottish/British Isles Music

Old Time/Mountain Music

Folk Music

Aural Tradition

Dance

Cajun Music and Zydeco

Court Music

Bluegrass Music

Jazz

Blues

Rock

New Age Music

Popular Music

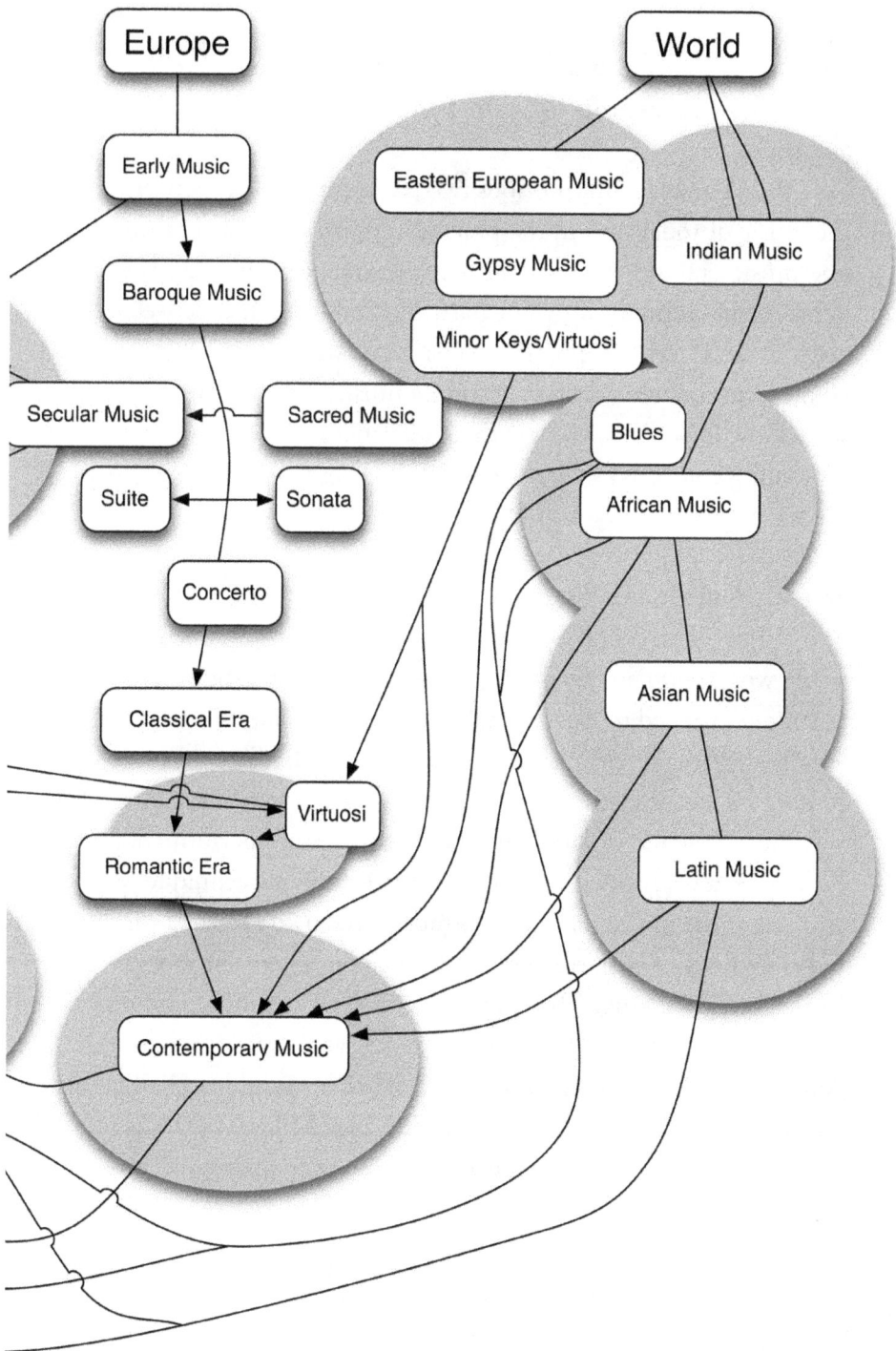

Europe

World

Early Music

Eastern European Music

Gypsy Music

Indian Music

Baroque Music

Minor Keys/Virtuosi

Secular Music ← Sacred Music

Blues

Suite ← → Sonata

African Music

Concerto

Classical Era

Asian Music

Virtuosi

Romantic Era

Latin Music

Contemporary Music

only a snapshot at a given time, with no claim for completeness. Each time I revisit this diagram I think of more connections and roots.

The Venn diagram (previous two pages) shows links between the music of today and in the past. It illustrates influences from one music era and style to another. Imaginary bridges are laid between the music of different parts of the world, and between classical and folk or popular music. As we explore specific connections between violin and fiddle music and their heritage, we will also look more closely at the similarities in the development of fiddling compared with the development of violin playing.

Baroque and Old-Time

When I first came to the United States and encountered the fiddle world, fiddlers would carefully explain to me the specific techniques needed to create a real fiddle feel and sound. At some length they made clear to me how different fiddling is from playing violin the classical way. What they really were explaining was the difference in technique between baroque performance technique and regular modern romantic violin technique! I witnessed that the violin hold was more relaxed and learned that old-time fiddlers in particular would speak of a circular motion in the actual bowing. That particular motion reminded me of the baroque bowing I had learned from Jaap Schröder at the Amsterdam conservatory. In his class Schröder would explicitly teach a circular motion, using gravity and natural weight to accompany the down-bow and lightness to accompany the up-bow. Another important similarity is the fiddling 'swing stroke' that reminds me of 'notes inégales' used in French baroque music. This is a case where different words describe the same technique.

Bluegrass

Bluegrass fiddlers also discussed their performance technique with me. Waltzes typically were played with some vibrato (a relaxed form) and longer bow strokes. In the faster bluegrass fiddle tunes an emphasis on virtuoso technique in the breaks or solos was not uncommon, including playing more in the higher positions. I was reminded of developments in violin history, as performance technique gradually moved away from the baroque to romantic ways of playing.

The Early Fiddle

"Fidel" or "vitula" in Latin means both strings as well as a stringed instrument. Its name evolved from "fidel" to "viola" (French *viole;* English *viol*) and the diminutive "violino." During the Medieval period (c.450-1450) these instruments were mainly used to accompany vocal music and play short instrumental passages (ritornellos=Italian for 'little return") between the verses. Different string instruments developed during the fifteenth and sixteenth centuries. One of the string instrument families was the lyre family. The "lira da braccio" (braccio=arm) was a forerunner of the violin. It had the characteristics of the earlier "fidel" as well as the later "violin." The actual violin developed in the mid-sixteenth century in Northern Italy. The violin quickly spread throughout Europe and was a popular instrument used both at the courts in Europe and on the streets.[43]

Dance Music

This brings us to the Baroque era in Europe. Dance music in the courts and on the streets developed into a very popular pastime for the people. Dance music played a major part in the development of later music both in the classical European music world and the popular folk-fiddle world. Everyone enjoyed dance forms such as the jig (gigue) at the courts, in villages, and in town centers. The popular square dance and contra dance find their roots in seventeenth-century English country dances. Geoffrey Hindley writes, "The interchange between folk and courtly music was considerable and many dances moved up in the social scale, so to speak, from the rumbustious [sic] and hot-blooded world of the village wedding or social celebration, to the more elegant, though scarcely less passionate, world of the court."[44]

Settlers

During the sixteenth and seventeenth centuries, following the explorers and subsequent traders, emigrants moved from Europe to North America. They brought with them their

---

[43] Metz, *Strijkinstrumenten Toen en Nu (String instruments Then and Now)*, Broekmans & van Poppel, 1974: 24-36.
[44] Geoffrey Hindley (edited by), "The Background To The Music" in *The Larousse Encyclopedia of Music* (London: Hamlyn, 1979): 157.

culture and music, such as fiddle music from the British Isles, Scotland, Ireland and from other countries, such as Poland and Germany. *Fisher's Hornpipe* is an example of a tune that originated in Germany.[45] Fiddle music was a rich culture in those days and was passed on from generation to generation by way of the aural tradition.

With this passing on of traditional fiddle tunes came the passing on of fiddle technique. This technique originated in Europe. Playing for dances brings with it a very strong realization of a pulse or beat. Both in early music in Europe and in old-time fiddle music in the United States the dance was strongly represented. Therefore it stands to reason that in both music forms, the pulse was clearly defined.

European settlers spread throughout North America and picked up different influences during the course of time as they mingled with other immigrant populations. With the different influences came an exploration of new possibilities with the violin, similar to that in Europe within the classical music world. This exploration led to effects that are very typical for the instrument such as the expansion of the regular tuning in fifths to different tunings. In the baroque era this was called "scordatura." Among fiddlers this is referred to as "cross-tuning." A particular African-American influence would be the "blue note," popular both in old-time music and in later bluegrass music.[46]

[45] Debby McClatchy, *Appalachian Traditional Music, A Short History, The Magazine for Traditional Music throughout the world*, 2000 Article MT055 http://www.mustrad.org.uk/articles/appalach.htm, accessed May 6, 2015.
46 Leslie Blake Price, *Bluegrass Nation: A Historical and Cultural Analysis of America's Truest Music*, Trace: Tennessee Research and Creative Exchange, Chancellor's Honors Thesis, 2011 http://trace.tennessee.edu/

Bluegrass Fiddling

In the early twentieth century the migration of people continued bringing an expansion of new influences. America flourished with its development of various musical styles, such as Dixieland, jazz, and blues. The fiddle world was influenced by the different characteristics of these musical styles. Jazz musicians such as Joe Venuti influenced bluegrass musicians. According to Chris Haigh, "He was probably the first violinist to popularize the "double shuffle" (a 123,123, 123,123,12,12 pattern rocking across two or three strings, and extending across two or more bars) which was quickly adopted by western swing and later bluegrass fiddlers."[47] The increasing popularity of radio and records helped spread different virtuoso techniques, including those from Austrian classical violinist Fritz Kreisler (1875-1962), and French jazz violinist Stephane Grapelli (1908-1997).

With the technical help of microphones there was not a great focus on playing strong and loud, as had been necessary in the bigger concert halls where classical music was predominantly performed. A bluegrass fiddler could focus on high speed passages with a great drive in tempo, which was very popular in this style of music. Another development to support the bluegrass way of playing was to extend the possibilities on the fingerboard of the instrument by using higher positions. Texas fiddling, Western Swing music, and the slower waltzes gave fiddlers an impetus to use longer bow strokes and vibrato.

cgi/viewcontent.cgi?article=2472&context=utk_chanhonoproj, page 9, accessed May 7, 2015.

[47] Chris Haigh, *Fiddling around the World,* http://www.fiddlingaround. co.uk/jazz/joe%20venuti.html, accessed April 13, 2015.

These are some examples of interconnecting influences of different musical styles and the historical periods as shown on the Venn diagram. I see a separate yet similar development in fiddling as in violin performance technique through the ages. I see though that indeed there are differences in development, like the ones based on physical circumstances. Violinists focus on sound production and projection to be heard without amplification in large concert halls. Fiddlers don't have the same need to develop a strong sound projection because they use microphones and electric sound enhancements to project or transmit their sound. Hence there is an opportunity to focus even more on the relaxed bow-use and wrist movement in fiddle music.

Virtuoso Solos in Bluegrass and Romantic Music

Moving away from playing solely dance tunes, bluegrass bands played for large audiences, similar to jazz bands. Bluegrass fiddle music developed an emphasis on virtuoso improvised solos or "breaks." These solos, highlighting a fiddler's creative mastery of the instrument, can be found in cadenzas that are part of European romantic violin concertos. However, unlike the improvised solos of bluegrass fiddlers, the cadenzas in European romantic and contemporary classical music tend to be composed, rather than improvised, by the composer or by a master-violinist.

Bridges

Throughout many centuries, bridges have been built between different musical worlds, for example, between folk and classical music, or between secular and sacred music. In the Renaissance and Baroque eras in Europe this resulted in compositions that embraced dance forms in both the folk music world as well as in music performed at the courts. The "suite" was a popular format used by composers in the Baroque era. Including the allemande, courante, and gigue, the dances at the court were not unlike the square and contra dances I have observed in the United States. The American dances typically were accompanied by a band playing fiddle music. John Holenko traces the influence of European dances on American dances:

> *At the end of the seventeenth century, English country dances were taken up by French dance masters. The French called these dances contra-dances or contredanses. As time progressed, these dances returned to England and were spread and reinterpreted in the United States.*[48]

Many composers have reached out to folk music for inspiration. Early composers such as William Byrd (c.1540-1623) wrote dances that were somewhat courtlier than folk music. Johann Sebastian Bach (1685-1750) composed dances in his cello suites and partitas for violin solo. Famous examples in the Romantic era are *Hungarian Dances* by Johannes Brahms (1833-1897), *Slavonic Dances* by Antonin Dvorak (1841-

---

[48] John Holenko, *Contra Dance Encyclopedia*, Mel Bay Publications, 2010: 6.

1904), and *Polovetsian Dances* by Alexander Borodin (1833-1887), and the twentieth- century ballet *Rodeo* and orchestral suite *Appalachian Spring* by Aaron Copland (1900-1990). The pulse of the dance stayed intact but the compositions were typically much more complex. It is interesting to see how the folk dances were incorporated into classical music from the time of the contra-dances at the courts and the baroque suites, to symphonic works in the Romantic era, to music of today. These connections represent bridges between the different styles.

Mark O'Connor: Contemporary Violinist, Fiddler, Composer, Bridge Builder

Currently, Mark O'Connor, a fiddler hailed for his virtuoso style and rich explorations of music, is building bridges by reaching out to the classical world. In 1997 he composed and performed a fiddle concerto and double violin concerto with orchestra, performing with violinist Nadja Salerno-Sonnenberg. In 1999 he formed a trio with cellist YoYo Ma and Edgar Meyer recording CDs with original music. Many other top classical musicians have played with him. With his virtuoso technique O'Connor explores music and opens up new horizons for us. His improvised concerto for violin solo and orchestra from 2010 completely removes all borders between musical styles.

The Appalachia Waltz

In 2000 President Clinton remarked about Mark O'Connor's composition *The Appalachia Waltz*: "It is one of the most important pieces of American music in many, many years, uniting the strains of classical music with American hill country music, which is an important part of my heritage."[49]

The *Appalachia Waltz* is a piece of tremendous beauty that I enjoy listening to as well as performing. Is it classical or is it a different style? It is American and is serene in its beauty. I find myself playing it, on occasion, in a free manner–taking it "away from the sheet" as per James Kelly. It matters not what style of music it is. A bridge was built. Its singing beauty, simplicity and complexity unites the styles and encompasses what is American music.

O'Connor's free style of playing includes a highly sophisticated violin technique as well as fabulous fiddle licks. He is a virtuoso musician and great ambassador of the idea of being open and flexible, recognizing the depth and beauty of music and exploring all musical styles.

The New American Violin Method
by Mark O'Connor

In the fall of 2009 Mark O'Connor published a new violin method. This multi-volume method underscores the importance of embracing different musical styles while starting off as a beginning violin or fiddle player. Indeed, by immediately integrating the different styles of playing and

---

[49] Bill Clinton, *Mark O'Connor web site*, http://markoconnor.com/index. php?page=quotes&family=quotes, accessed April 11, 2015.

learning all musical elements that are involved with this, one is more likely to become an all-round musician who is free to choose whatever style of music she/he wants to play. In his violin method O'Connor welcomes the idea that, when trained well, any violinist can cross the bridge from one style to another.

The Bridge: Summary of Similarities and Differences

Below are four charts, covering similarities and differences. I noted that there are similarities between bluegrass fiddle and classical violin. I also noted that when it comes to differences between fiddle and baroque violin, these would also be differences between fiddle and classical violin. Most similarities can be found between fiddle and baroque violins.

Similarities

Fiddle – Baroque Violin

Fiddle	Baroque Violin	Chapter	Page
Posture: violin hold: Violin slightly down, more relaxed	similar	I. Old Time Fiddlers II. Baroque Performance Technique II. Posture, Holding the violin…	34 61-62 62-64
Shoulder rest not always used	Similar (not yet invented)	I. Old Time Fiddlers II. Posture, Holding the violin…	34 62-64
Chin rest not always used	similar	II. Posture, Holding the violin…	63
Posture: bow hold Higher up the bow, not necessarily at the frog	similar	I. Old Time Fiddlers II. Posture, Holding the violin… II. Bows and Bow-Holds IV. Baroque and Old-Time	34 64/65 67/68 126
Small bow strokes	similar	I. Old Time Fiddlers	34
Relaxed sound	similar	V. A teacher's journey IV. Interpretation of Baroque Music in the Romantic Era	145 116
"down-ups"	"rule of the down bow" downbow on the beat	II. A circular motion	65
similar	Natural weight/ gravity in bowing	II. Posture, Bowing, Chin- and Shoulder-rest, Gravity	64/65
similar	Downbow heavier than upbow	II. A Circular Motion IV. Intertwining Action and Re-Action: The Story of Builders, Composers and Performers	65/66 105-108

Circle motion in bowing	Similar: Circular motion	II. A circular motion IV. Baroque and Old-Time	65/66 126
Loose Wrist	Similar (Vivaldi passages for instance)	II. Loose Wrist III. Byron Berline	66/67 88
Swing Stroke	Notes inégales	II. Notes Inegales or Swing strokes IV. Baroque and Old-Time	73-74 127
Little (or no) vibrato	similar	II. Vibrato	76-78
Fiddle tunes – dances: binary form	Dances in suites: binary form	II. Dance Music: Gigue and Jig	58-61
Playing for square dances Jig – dance music	Playing for court dances / suite Gigue (suite) dance music	II. Dance music –The gigue and the Jig IV. Dance music IV. Bridges V. Rhythm and Timing	58-61 128 132 159
Strong rhythm/ pulse	similar	IV. Settlers V. Rhythm and Timing	129 159
Improvisation	Freedom and improvisational skill Improvisation over a long note (cadenza)	V. Chord structure and Improvisation IV. Cadenzas – Improvised in Baroque Music; Composed in Classical, Romantic, 20th century Violin Concertos	158 117/118
Cross tuning	Scordatura	II. Scordatura or Cross Tuning IV. Settlers	75/76 129
similar	Use of modes	II. Modes	55-58
Regional interpretations of tunes	Rhetoric/ ornamentations country specific	II. Music rhetoric	71/72

Similarities

Bluegrass Fiddle – Classical Violin

Bluegrass Fiddle	Violin	Chapter	Page
More use of longer bow strokes than in Old time fiddle	More use of longer bow strokes than in baroque violin	IV. Bluegrass	127
Vibrato in slower tunes, like waltzes	Vibrato in most music, but for (less so) Early/baroque music	IV. Bluegrass IV. Bluegrass Fiddling	127 131
Virtuoso technique, especially in solos	Virtuoso technique, especially in concertos and cadenzas	IV. Bluegrass IV. Virtuoso Solos	127 131/132
Higher up the fingerboard	Similar	IV. Bluegrass Fiddling	131

Differences

Fiddle – Baroque and Classical Violin

Fiddle	Violin	Chapter	Page
Set up: rosin on the instrument Flatter bridge for some fiddlers	Set up: careful handling of instrument and the varnish	I. The need for immersion V. Overcoming Obstacles	44 146
Georgia Bow and other strokes (patterns), accentuating off beat	Bowing indicated, after careful consideration – exact reproduction	I. Byron Berline V. Overcoming Obstacles	50/51 147
Shuffle stroke specific to fiddling		II. Old Joe Clark	72
Double shuffle		III. Berline Tips IV. Bluegrass Fiddling	89 130
Improvised back up Chop on back beat	Accompaniment – sheet music	I. Holding back I. The need for immersion III. Lewis' Tips III. Bright's Tips	40/41 44 91 93

Blue note – African-American influence		III. BerlineTips IV. Settlers	88 129/130
Aural tradition	Sheet music/ composed music	I. The Aural Tradition – A New Experience III. The Aural Tradition V. Aural Learning	35/36 81/82 156/157
Original "in the moment" tunes	Exact renditions	I. The Aural Tradition – A New Experience	36
Instant analysis in jam sessions	Sheet music	III. The Aural Tradition	81/82
Fiddle tunes – sheet music = one interpretation; now make it your own	Sheet music: composers intention interpreted	III. "Let The Tune Live Away From The Sheet!" - James Kelly	84/85
Knowledge bank of licks and chords	Sheet music / studies / scales	I. Recording Jam Sessions and Studying Fiddle and Violin I. The need for immersion III. Berline Tips	36 44/45 88
Improvisation over chord structure	Focus on melody	III. Key and Chord Progressions III. Berline Tips IV. Interpreting the Composed Piece: Melody Line and Harmonic Structure V. Chord structure and Improvisation	80/81 88 120/121 158
Underlying harmonic structure important	Focus on melodic line	IV. Interpreting the Composed Piece and the Harmonic Structure II.Chord Structure and Improvisation	120 158

Differences

Fiddle and Classical Violin

Fiddle	Violin	Chapter	Page
Often no shoulder rest	Most often use of shoulder rest	II. Posture, Holding the violin…	63/64
Small bow strokes	Tone development – big strokes for full sound	V. Teaching Fiddle to Violin Students	152
Circular motion: Downbow heavier than up-bow	Down- and up-bow are compatible	II. A Circular Motion III. Berline Tips IV. Intertwining Action and Re-Action: The Story of Builders, Composers and Performers	65/66 88 105-107
Relaxed sound	Bow technique to "fill the hall"	IV. Vibrato and sound projection V. Teaching Fiddle to Violin Students	116 152
Little (or no) vibrato in Old-Time; Bluegrass includes vibrato	Vibrato	IV. Vibrato and sound projection	115/116
Short tunes	Often lengthy and complex compositions	V. Introduction	142
Rubato not typical	Rubato	IV. Rubato vs Strict Timing V. Rhythm and Timing	101 159
In Bluegrass: drive – high speed passages, while relaxed sound (microphones) More emphasis on loose wrist	High speed passages with need for projection	IV. Bluegrass Fiddling	131
Improvisation in breaks or solos	Cadenzas in concertos composed	IV. Cadenzas, Improvised in Baroque Music; Composed in Classical, Romantic, 20th-century Violin Concertos	117-119

Chapter 5
Moving Forward: The Teacher's Role:
Turning Experience Into Philosophy[50]

S imilar to violin playing, fiddling encompasses different styles of music. Performance technique differs depending on the style of music being played. Increasingly a wider variety of violin techniques are required to play fiddle music. For example, the bow is used in more varied ways to accommodate the improvisational aspects of bluegrass fiddling. Speed and more regular use of positions support the popularity of virtuoso "licks" (short melodic phrase) and "breaks" (solos) by bluegrass fiddlers. Vibrato is more commonly used in fiddle styles other than old-time. Further, as fiddling incorporates blues and jazz elements a fully-fledged and advanced violin technique is expected.

---

[50] According to Merriam-Webster Thesaurus, Philosophy is a "set of ideas about how to do something or how to live. "
From http://www.merriam-webster.com/dictionary/philosophy

It is intriguing to see how over time, music has moved from the baroque language to new horizons and possibilities for exploration. Composers and performers have interacted and invented new avenues. New techniques supported new compositions. New compositions, in turn, required new techniques. Violin virtuosi like Niccolò Paganini (1782-1840) and Fritz Kreisler (1875-1962) made major breakthroughs in the treatment and versatility of the instrument. In Jazz, the great master Stéphane Grapelli (1908-1997) has been very influential and paved the way for other great violinists, including violin and fiddle virtuoso Mark O'Connor (b.1961). These violinists are some of the finest musicians who have added to the violin and fiddle repertoire, technique and style.

After considering the different elements that constitute a comparison between violin and fiddle traditions, questions remain. If the violin and the fiddle are the same instrument, then why are violinists and fiddlers so separated? Is it because of the technique used? Is it because of the music—lengthy and often complicated compositions versus short 'tunes'? Is it because of improvisation? What about the difference between learning from sheet music versus the aural tradition?

As teachers, we can contemplate these questions and bring about change in the depth of teaching our young musicians of the future. Violinists can join fiddlers in the versatility of improvisation and the freedom of interpretation. Likewise, fiddlers can strengthen their performance fundamentals by exploring classical violin techniques and incorporating these techniques into traditional fiddle music.

I believe we all stand to gain by embracing music holistically and by seeking to minimize the compartmentalization between different styles of music. The language of music is universal. We can learn to expand our musical horizon and be open to the nuances of the style and musicians who differ from our own.

Readiness

The task of a teacher is to prepare the student for playing music, by way of mastering the instrument. Huge strides can be made if a teacher is willing and able to give the most open approach to music. A teacher's role involves sending the student into the world with a *readiness to learn* and to play any kind of music they wish, recognizing that students may have preferences for particular musical styles that may differ from the teacher's preference. The teacher must also equip the student to be an independent musician who will, in turn, share their gift with the world.

I am a classically trained violinist with a specialization in baroque violin. My journey in music has given me a chance to venture out to fiddling of all kinds. My leanings may be swing and some jazz, as it reminds me of what I heard in my youth. However, old-time and bluegrass fiddling seemed more foreign to my personal heritage. As such, I had to struggle to learn the feel of fiddling. Improvisation and backup with a natural sense of chord progressions were difficult to learn. My path was not smoothly paved, but it also installed the belief in me that it would have made a substantial difference if fiddling and improvisation had been a part of my violin training from the start.

Teachers can build the bridges that will allow their students to be ready to participate in the world of *any* style of music. Teachers can provide a more encompassing musical background for their students by exploring the variety of music available, studying the techniques and noting their similarities and differences. Both fiddlers and violinists can be supported in their educations by exposure to the rich variety of musical styles and techniques available.

I see the different musical worlds of violin and fiddle playing, separate and yet bound together by shared roots. I see the interconnectedness of the different musical styles as indicated on the Venn diagram ("Circles"). I see a great reason to bridge the apparent gap between the violin and fiddle world of performance and education, without concern for losing the particular performance technique belonging to the style of music one choses to play.

Immersion

In order to really learn to play and understand *any* style of music it is important to immerse yourself in that music by way of playing in ensembles, orchestras, bands, or by participating in jam sessions. Nothing can replace getting 'the feel' for playing a particular musical style than simply getting out there and playing, listening, and learning. The musical expression and deep sense of style comes with time and cannot be matched by formal lessons. Each complements the other, enriching the student's foundation in the world of music.

Overcoming Obstacles

While we may specialize in fiddle or violin music we can also provide more versatile training to our students. A fiddler can learn to play violin and a violinist can learn to play fiddle. Bridges can be formed and we can recognize that we all play the same instrument. Adjustments can be made to the instrument, but a violin is a violin and no different from a fiddle.

How interesting it is then, that I have been witness to off-hand remarks from fiddlers and violinists alike, each putting down the efforts of the other. Because my experiences are not unique, I will address these comments. With every comment, I hope to break down the walls that separate these similar musical worlds and use those bricks to build bridges.

OBSTACLE: To play baroque music in the baroque style, one needs to use an instrument that is fully "baroque fitted," including a shorter neck, "gut" strings, etc. The tuning needs to be different, that is A = 415 Hz versus the common modern tuning of A = 440 Hz (or even higher).

BRIDGE: If baroque music was to be played using only baroque violins, very few people would still be able to enjoy this music. However interesting and desirable it may be to use baroque violins and play in baroque tuning, everyone can play baroque music with the sparkle and deeper intent and emotion of the wonderful compositions of the Baroque era. The one very important element is indeed, that one must be taught. If a baroque piece is played in a romantic fashion, the music stands a great chance to lose its character and excitement. Timing, phrasing, rhetoric, and understanding the expression of the music all combine to the tools a good musician can use to give a moving and exciting performance of baroque music.

OBSTACLE: To play fiddle, you must have the instrument set up like a fiddle, e.g., with a flatter bridge, and steel strings.

BRIDGE: Are we to have three different instruments (modern violin, baroque violin, and a violin set up for fiddling) if we wish to play music in these different styles? Wow! How impractical. Let us not limit ourselves or our students if the instrument that is owned does not exactly meet the exact specifications of the specialist. Enjoy the music!

OBSTACLE: Playing old-time music is really simple; it is for beginners; very little is played in positions if any at all. No vibrato is required. The tunes are simple melodies that repeat endlessly. The keys are easy (few sharps and flats). Very little technique is needed.

BRIDGE: While it is true that the actual melody can be acquired easily by a beginner because the tune itself has a certain simplicity, that is just the starting point. Some old-time musicians may add a host of notes to "fill in" the melody. Others may add rhythm in their bowing by way of accentuating the "off-beat". Open strings may be added as a drone as well as double stops, to add color and texture to the melody. Then, all of a sudden, what appeared simple is no longer simple. A lot of improvisation and subtle "feel" of the style is required when playing the old-time way. Abundant repetition befits old-time fiddlers as they play for dances and gatherings, oftentimes with little or no accompaniment.

OBSTACLE: Playing baroque music is really simple. It is for beginners. Very little is played in positions, if any at all. Very little vibrato (or none) is required. The melody is simple. The keys are simple (few sharps and flats). Very little technique is needed.

BRIDGE: Baroque music originated long ago. It is interesting how through the ages taste and culture defined what way to play baroque music. There are recordings from top notch soloists in the early twentieth century that display tempi totally out of touch with the intention of the composer. The pulse is incredibly important in this style of music having major roots in dance music. Ornamentation, baroque bowing technique and left hand technique help make the music bright and expressive. To perform solo Bach such as the *Chaconne* requires a good solid technique of a virtuoso nature combined with great musicality and a good understanding of baroque performance and expression.

OBSTACLE: Violinists have no loose wrist and their vibrato is too fast. They play too rigidly; too square.

BRIDGE: A loose wrist is part of the basic violin technique required to be a good violinist. However, one doesn't always apply a loose wrist in violin playing. A violinist is more likely involved in giving a carefully articulated rendition of a tune, which includes a very precise treatment of every note. The swing stroke (uneven notes) for instance is barely used in classical music. The more all-round a violinist is, however, the more familiar he will be with this interpretation of passages. Baroque violinists have that particular style of bowing in their repertoire. A violinist in good command of technique will have vibrato of varying speeds.

OBSTACLE: A fiddler has only some elementary technique and no refined sound production. It would be hilarious if they tried to play classical music.

BRIDGE: Byron Berline once said to me, with a smile:

If I were to read music and attempt to play classical music, you would have a hard time with me, because I would never play something the same way twice and I would have a hard time following the exact guidelines indicated on the sheet music.

How true a statement! One can expect a fiddler to be an artist in improvisation to the point where playing exactly what is on the page is very difficult for him or her. Can they apply themselves to do so? Of course! All it takes is interest in it and being introduced to the language of classical music.

A Teacher's Journey

As a violinist and violin teacher I have had the opportunity to meet many different students and musicians. I have heard a wealth of musical styles and played in a wide variety of venues. These experiences have led me to formulate ideas that constitute a personal philosophy which continues to be fluid and open to change.

Fletcher Bright, fiddle, with Tom Rozum on mandolin at a bluegrass workshop at Augusta Heritage Center of Davis & Elkins College, West Virginia, 1993

In the Netherlands my students had asked me to teach not only classical violin, but different styles of music as well. On my first venture to the United States I researched bluegrass fiddling, immersing myself in fiddling by participating in jam sessions and taking fiddle lessons. I participated in local and national fiddle contests, and attended fiddle workshops with a number of great fiddle masters including Byron Berline, Fletcher Bright, Laurie Lewis (Bluegrass) and James Kelly (Irish). Also I participated in workshops given by a number of great old-time and other fiddlers.

Interestingly, at these jam sessions, workshops and festivals, I noticed that fiddlers shared their art of fiddling as if it was a unique style, completely unlike violin playing. Old-time fiddlers explained to me, in their unique musical terms, how to bow and what other aspects were specific to their musicianship. It felt as if I had no background with the instrument. Surprisingly, though, it brought to mind the baroque violin lessons I had taken at the Conservatory in Amsterdam!

Since immigrating to the United States I have expanded my professional music horizon to include the teaching of fiddle as well as violin, and explored fiddle repertoire and performance technique in depth.

Teaching Fiddle to Violin Students

Gradually I began to realize that fiddle music could have similar roots as violin music because I had noticed great similarities between fiddle and baroque violin performance techniques. I started giving workshops for my violin students, comparing the two, and exploring many existing styles of fiddle music, including old-time, bluegrass, Western Swing, Cajun, and Irish.

Annemieke's fiddle workshop with students at Paynes
Prairie, Gainesville, Florida, 1993

Between 2004 and 2006 I had the opportunity to teach fiddle at a middle school in Gainesville. My students had the opportunity to participate in the Sawgrass Fiddle Contest. As part of my teaching curriculum I used video and audio recordings to introduce the children to the fiddle world. After this initial introduction, students were given the opportunity to sign up for my fiddle class.

The students had different violin backgrounds, ranging from no lessons to having had regular private lessons for many years. Some were talented members of the local youth orchestra. It was energizing to work with these young musicians. They eagerly followed my directions and learned to play a fiddle tune or two, mostly by way of using sheet music. I also worked with the group, teaching them fiddle tunes by ear, bit by bit, phrase by phrase, as I had learned in fiddle workshops.

During this period I was well aware of the special care I needed to take in order not to interfere with their personal violin technique, as taught by their violin teachers. Under no circumstance did I wish to confuse the students' already learned violin technique. I taught tunes, their musical expression, and simple technical instructions focusing on rhythm, taking small bow strokes for particular songs, and creating an overall more relaxed sound.

No matter how carefully I approached the fiddle class, after a while—invariably—a student would say he or she couldn't continue. When I asked for the reason, I learned that the private teacher didn't care for fiddling, or was concerned about the student being held back in technique by learning "bad habits." The particular student might just have worked on tone development and projection, using big bow strokes. Therefore, the bowing technique I shared, including short bow strokes, might have been perceived as contradictory to their conventional bowing. Short and long bow strokes each require different technique, and both are important to learn.

I was saddened to learn of the student's reluctance to stay in the fiddle class. This hesitation illustrated my experience as a violinist and violin teacher trying to promote fiddling among young musicians. Students who came to my studio were offered the choice to learn violin, fiddle or a combination of both. Outside my studio I found that teachers would usually not introduce fiddling to their students. Tunes of *The Fairfield Fiddle Farm* books by Charles A. Hall— part of the accepted repertoire within the Suzuki curriculum—were the exception.

My learning about this limitation in exploring fiddling caused me to wonder. If fiddling is so much fun, especially for young budding musicians, and fiddling is so much a part of the heritage and culture of the United States, then why are violin teachers not more inclined to absorb fiddling into their curricula? This is a question I have struggled with since arriving in the United States in 1990.

The first thought that comes to mind is that violin teachers were not taught how to play or teach non-classical styles. In 1990 I seemed a lone voice in the American classical world doing research in a non-classical style, i.e., fiddling. But times have changed since I came to the States. Not only is the concert podium enriched by fabulous string players who perform a mix of musical styles, but also teachers appear to be more open to the wide variety of styles. A few years ago I asked various teachers in north central Florida to consider sending their students to a camp that offered a great variety of styles, with a focus on fiddling. I was delighted to get positive responses, for example: "*The camp sounds great! Maybe sometime in the future I would be able to attend myself.*"

The Sawgrass Fiddle Contest

In 1998 a group of close friends and I started a new organization called the Sawgrass Fiddle Association to promote fiddling among young musicians. The annual focus of the association was a contest and workshops for children and teens, serving as an introduction for families to fiddling and the folk music world. Contact was made with the local violin community and the wider music world of Florida and Georgia. It was greeted with some hesitation. Some positive remarks were made in respect to our endeavor, but few violin students entered the contest.

Again I wondered: *"Why such hesitation?"* One day when I shared some of my surprise and disappointment a colleague gave me a very helpful insight: *"It is hard to support a student in a style of playing that one (the teacher) knows little about."* This was a very fair statement. I started to think about that simple and straightforward remark and felt it needed more exploration.

A New Role: Violin/Fiddle Instructor

How do teachers support students in styles of playing about which the teachers know little? So far I had not considered this lack of knowledge to be an actual stumbling block. I had assumed teachers here in the United States, where fiddling is so active, would have more understanding of American non-classical music. Surely, they could find supporting materials if they so wished. If it wasn't their choice to teach it, they could consult with or refer to fiddle teachers. Indeed, if a different style of playing the violin *could* be offered to their students, would they embrace the opportunity? Accordingly, I had offered fiddle workshops as a courtesy to violin students in the area, to help bridge the gap between classical and fiddle styles and to increase participation in the Sawgrass Fiddle Contest and workshops. I opened participation to students and teachers, believing that teachers would relish the opportunity to expand their own musical world.

Unfortunately, I was facing an apparent lack of enthusiasm and a clear hesitancy among violin educators, but I didn't give up. Originally, I came to the United States to learn about fiddling and to bring this newly acquired understanding back to the Netherlands to share with my students and colleagues there. Now, it became clear to me that there was, and is, ample opportunity for me to play an active role in promoting the tradition of fiddling among violinists and young violin students in the United States. This would help to broaden their perspective and horizon of the violin world and of American music.

Studying fiddle in the United States made me realize how this music is an integral part of the overall culture. Fiddling is such a vibrant part of the musical heritage that I cannot imagine playing the violin and not incorporating this style of music. I also learned firsthand how enriching it is to explore more than one style when learning to play an instrument.

Learning to play fiddle tunes—both simple and more advanced contest tunes—was a very exciting process. I went places with my instrument I had not gone before, including improvisation and learning to play a tune by ear following the aural tradition. A number of aspects involved with this process show the importance of incorporating fiddling into the violin curriculum.

Aural Learning

Aubrey Haynie showing Annemieke some licks at
a bluegrass festival in Florida, 1991

Why learn by ear if you can read music? Typically, when learning from sheet music, my very first action would be to "read through" the tune. I would slowly make my way playing through the whole melody and familiarize myself with the notes. At a later stage, I would look at the tune in more detail. However, I would stay very connected to the image of the sheet music and depended on it. After knowing how to play the whole tune, I would set out to memorize it. My dependency of the sheet music was hard to shed.

Now, learning a tune aurally, phrase by phrase without looking at the page, I forced myself to access a different part of my brain to deepen my understanding of each phrase, lick and turn. A fascinating and exciting process, yet not easy at first, especially not if the other way was so much easier to access! It was hard not to feel tempted to sight-read through the tune as a whole.

I focused on the characteristics of the phrases, notes, rhythm, and musical line. It was indeed a difficult process for me as I was new to it. However, I believe that this experience and the many times since then that I learned new material by ear, has helped me greatly. It helped me to assess the depth, the feel and intent of the music. This experience enriched my musicality and ability to play in a variety of ways. I am very grateful that I had the opportunity to take this route and, indeed, to teach my students to become versatile and learn music by way of reading, as well as in the aural tradition, right from the start.

Why should it matter to introduce other musical styles to violin students all over the world? This broad question warrants looking at violin playing from a number of different vantage points. Realizing this, I started to look further into the question, starting with two main aspects of music: chord structure, and rhythm and timing. Strengthening the awareness and application of these two aspects are very important to a thorough study of the violin.

Chord Structure and Improvisation

By not restricting yourself to one style of violin playing, the overall ability to express yourself musically is infinitely improved. A violinist becomes a better musician if she/he has an understanding and feel of a given chord structure. Improvisation depends on that underlying harmonic structure. Within the baroque tradition a certain freedom and improvisational skill is expected of a violinist. This is not necessarily taught. However, it is expected that a harpsichordist or organist is able to construct an intricate accompaniment providing the harmonic structure underlying the melody when seeing *figured bass*, musical notation in which numbers indicate intervals or chords in relation to the bass line. The harpsichordist or organist learns to create a musical accompaniment of the melodic line(s), complete with improvised flourishes of notes. Likewise, a well-trained fiddle player can play a solo, improvising over a chord progression that is the basis of a fiddle tune. Typically, violinists focus on the melody without an active knowledge of the actual chord progression. The melodic notes are, however, based on chords and once the harmonic structures are learned, music can be played with an enriched depth and sense of understanding. Violinists will benefit greatly from studying harmonic structure, inviting a more in-depth expression of the melody - whether they play baroque repertoire or music of a later time period.

Rhythm and Timing

A good sense of rhythm is essential to the development of technique as well as the overall musical expression of the violinist. Since the violin is a melodic instrument, violinists tend to focus less on rhythm and more on the perfection of the melodic line. Often one can notice violinists playing with rubato, a degree of rhythmic and expressive freedom in the tempo within a melodic line. This is acceptable depending on the historical style period. Individual violinists may have a great sense of rhythm and timing, but on the whole they are not known for their ability to keep a steady tight rhythm.

Fiddling, on the other hand, thrives on tight rhythm or timing. One feels a very clear pulse and drive based on the provided beat. Fiddlers typically accompanied dances (square and contra dances) where the beat is of utmost importance. The best way to experience that is by actually playing for a dance oneself. When I was asked one day to play a waltz for a dance, I was instantly aware of the absolute need to keep the beat. I felt the people moving their feet and bodies to my music. It was an amazing experience I had not had before. It brought home to me the importance of keeping a good solid beat.

Playing for dances the way fiddlers do is much like the way musicians at European courts in the 1500s would play for the court dances. Here is another clear link between the heritage of fiddling and violin playing. Musicians played for people who danced, be they at European courts or American square and contra dances. Although the dances varied in tempo from slow to fast, in both cases there was an expectation of clear timing and tight rhythm to accommodate the dancers. As music moved away from the dance floor, it was free to evolve and include more emphasis on the melodic line and less on strict rhythm.

If teachers were open to various styles and music from different countries and historical eras, the musicianship of their students might increase tremendously. Their students could learn more about the harmonic structure (chords) and the flow (rhythm and timing) of music and would, themselves, be better musicians for it. Knowing the usual progressions of chords supports improvisation as well as improved sight-reading.

Enriched Musical Culture

If fiddling is not taught within the general curriculum of the beginning violinist, how can one expect young people to develop an interest in this rich musical culture? People build an interest in playing the violin typically based on their personal experiences. Their affinity with the instrument may come from family members or friends playing music, or from their wider environment of electronic media. They are connected to their musical environment and heritage. Teachers have the professional responsibility to be sensitive to their student's particular musical history. This knowledge of the student's background may influence the offered curriculum, if the teacher is able to vary the curriculum.

The violin is such an incredibly versatile instrument. Here is a chance to give students opportunities to explore new intellectual territory. If the curriculum is purely grounded in the classical repertoire, doors appear closed to learning other non-classical styles. The student's original interest in other styles may "dry up" with the student never experiencing fiddling. If fiddling is not included, it seems unlikely she/he will have a chance to appreciate this particular musical world and style of playing, and may stop playing altogether.

Jam Sessions and Festivals

Two violin students, Abigail Ward and Cassady Allen, participating in the Sawgrass twin-fiddle contest (image courtesy of Humberto Herrera)

Violin students may be invited to come to jam sessions or festivals. Concerts and music heard on radio, TV or in public places might also promote music that is part of the vast realm of the American musical heritage and culture. The computer and the internet play a great role in the connection young people have with music. It seems, though, that through these various experiences the student faces an actual disconnect between the music she/he hears around her/him and the music she/he is taught.

The violin teacher is pivotal to exposing the student to the richness of music, classical and non-classical. Classical music, if presented as *one* of the many musical styles, will find a more natural place in the student's field of interest.

At one point I was given the opportunity to represent the Sawgrass Fiddle Association to promote the annual fiddle contest for children and teens among the young string players of a local youth orchestra. This prestigious orchestra in the Gainesville area was fully classical in their setting and focus. Yet it seemed to me it would be easy to elicit excitement among its members to participate in a fiddle contest. Free workshops, offered by me, would help enhance this excitement. Being involved in workshops would not change the young person's general direction of becoming a classical violinist. It would merely be an enriching experience. Again I learned this was not automatically the case.

In my quest and in support of the Sawgrass Fiddle Association and contest, I wrote an article in the orchestra's newsletter discussing my point of view that fiddling is just a different style and can easily be approached as another learning experience. It would not jeopardize one's violin technique, but would add to it. There was no response to my article and workshop offer. I found out how these young aspiring violinists, who are classically trained, seem to have little interest in exploring and venturing out to fiddling. I suspect that an interest in fiddling would only be fueled by folk music influences outside the orchestra. Here, I witnessed a clear gap between the violin studios, the youth orchestras, and the fiddle and folk music world.

Broadening Musical Horizons

Do we listen to the requests of our students? It is interesting that students who come to my violin studio show great variety in their desire to learn the instrument and its repertoire. Some indeed have a particular notion of learning to play classical music. Such students tend to have a background that has given them exposure to the treasures of this musical style. Others come to my practice with a direct request to learn to play fiddle. Their heritage is more related to the fiddle and folk music world. Then, there are those in the middle who wish to learn to play the instrument and both classical and other music as it is presented. It is interesting to see how different each student is and how different their wishes are.

Personally, I cannot deny my heritage and training as a classical violinist. In my studio every student will be trained in classical technique, and they will learn to read music. However, I also introduce the students to different musical styles and the performance technique that suits the styles. For instance, I work on baroque violin performance technique as the student progresses and plays music from the Baroque era. Similarly I introduce fiddle tunes to every student and address some of the particular techniques that are inherent to fiddling.

Typically, students enjoy the other musical styles presented to them and benefit from the variety and diversity of technique and musical approaches. Some students will choose to stay in their original field of interest and others will be more likely to cross the bridge and return to their original path of interest. The ease by which they can switch gives me great satisfaction. Recently one classically focused student of mine used his baroque violin technique and overall knowledge to perform a fiddle tune most handsomely to a big audience. His performance was fabulous yet he insisted he played violin and not fiddle. It is my belief, therefore, that as teachers we have to be flexible in responding to our students' requests.

Fiddling Deserves to Live On in the Soul of the Nation

To connect to a musical heritage that is an integral part of the overall culture and vibrancy of the United States, violin teachers need to embrace opportunities to expose their students to this rich musical culture and encompass fiddling in their violin teaching practices. From studying fiddle I learned firsthand how enriching it can be to explore more than one musical style. The technical and musical versatility of a violinist can be greatly enriched by venturing out to many different musical styles. Throughout my personal exploration period, I practiced fiddle and even participated in a few fiddle contests, such as the Florida State Fiddlers Contest and the Grand Masters Fiddle Contest in Nashville, Tennessee.

Florida State Fiddle Contest, White Springs, Florida, 1992

Grand Master Fiddle Championship with "Wild"
Bill Leyel, Nashville, Tennessee, 1992

It was an exciting experience, in particular because I explored things with my instrument that I had not done before, including improvisation and learning by listening—the aural tradition. I came across a number of facets that together made a clear case for incorporating the fiddle repertoire and traditions in the violin studio curriculum. It became very clear to me how enriching this can be! This was reason enough for me to explore this connection further.

How Fiddling Helps Classical-Romantic Violinists

The focus on chord progression and tight rhythm or timing in fiddling is very helpful for violinists to acquire. But there are other areas. While observing fiddlers play, it became clear to me that fiddling helps the violin student technically and musically. The repetition of simple melodies, improvising on these, flexibility in the wrist, and freedom of interpretation are elements of fiddling that enrich the regular violin curriculum. It is my direct experience that working on these and learning tunes in the aural tradition give the student a fresh and enriched musical understanding.

My Musical Journey: A Bridge

Looking back on my journey from my roots as a violinist specialized in baroque music in Amsterdam, I see how curiosity led me to explore the deeper value of music in life. I found meaning in music therapy which helped me see how music is a means of communication. I stumbled over the art of improvisation and found recognition in the technique used by old-time fiddlers.

I started to realize how opening one to the world of fiddling, one's own world of violin playing became incredibly enriched. I saw walls built by violinists and fiddlers alike, yet I also saw how bridges could be built with the materials ready at hand.

In the course of writing this book, I am excited about how bridges are being built by some amazing musicians. I enjoy the wonderful diverse world of music played on the violin. I hope this book will help bring down walls, and bridge gaps that may have arisen.

Bibliography

Books and Journals

Babitz, Sol. *"Notes Inegales": A Communication.* Journal of the American Musicological Society, Vol. 20, No. 3 1967: 473-476.

Leslie Blake Price, *Bluegrass Nation: A Historical and Cultural Analysis of America 's Truest Music,* Trace: Tennessee Research and Creative Exchange, Chancellor's Honors Thesis, 2011, http://trace.tennessee.edu/cgi/viewcontent.cgi?article=2472&context=utk_chanhonoproj, page 9, accessed May 7, 2015.

Brody, David. *The Fiddler's Fake Book.* Oak Publications, 1983.

Carre, Anthoine. *Livre de Pieces de Guitarre et de Musique.* www.donaldsauter.com/antoine-carre.htm, accessed May 8, 2015.

Clinton, Bill. *Mark O'Connor.* markoconnor.com/index.php?page=quotes&family=quotes, accessed April 11, 2015.

Consort, The Alachua. www.alachuaconsort.com, accessed May 5, 2015.

Consort & Players, Gabrieli. *The Monteverdi Violins.* www.themonteverdiviolins.org/baroque-violin.html, accessed May 5, 2015.

Editors of Encyclopedia Britannica. *"Church modes - Ecclesiastical Mode",* Encyclopedia Britannica, www.britannica.com/EBchecked/topic/117215/church-mode, accessed May 7, 2015.

Gable, Frederick K. *"Some Observations concerning Baroque and Modern Vibrato"*. Performance Practice Review, Claremont, scholarship.claremont.edu/cgi/viewcontent.cgi?article=1105&context=ppr, accessed May 6, 2015.

Chris Haigh, *Fiddling around the World*, http://www.fiddlingaround.co.uk/jazz/joe%20venuti.html, accessed April 13, 2015.

Harnoncourt, Nikolaus. *Baroque Music Today: Music As Speech: Ways to a New Understanding of Music*. Amadeus Press, 1995.

Hindley, Geoffrey (edited by). *The Larousse Encyclopedia of Music*. Hamlyn,1979.

Holenko, John. *Contra Dance Encyclopedia*. Mel Bay Publications, 2010.

Kuijken, Filip. *Construction and Repair of Violins – Violas – Cellos / Baroque, Classic and Modern* www.kuijkenviolins.com/baclamo/, accessed May 5, 2015.

Kuntz, Andrew. *The Fiddler's Companion – "A Descriptive Index of North American, British Isles and Irish Music for the Folk Violin and other Instruments"*, www.ibiblio.org/fiddlers/index.html, accessed April13, 2015.

McClatchy, Debby. *"Appalachian Traditional Music, A Short History"*, *The Magazine for Traditional Music Throughout the World*. 2000 Article MT055 www.mustrad.org.uk/articles/appalach.htm, accessed May 6, 2015.

Metz, Louis. *Strijkinstrumenten Vroeger en Nu (String instruments Then and Now)*. Broekmans & van Poppel, 1974.

Neumann, Frederic. "*The Vibrato Controversy*", Performance Practice Review, Claremont scholarship.claremont.edu/cgi/viewcontent.cgi?article=1058&context=ppr, accessed May 6, 2015.

Sachs, Curt. *Geschiedenis der Muziek (Our Musical Heritage: A Short History of Music)*. Het Spectrum, 1973. (New York, NY: Prentice-Hall, Inc. 1955).

Schröder, Jaap. *Bach's Solo Violin Works–A Performer's Guide*. New Haven, CT: Yale University Press, 2007.

Thomas, Stephen and Erlewine, Rovi. *On line biography of Bill Monroe*, www.billboard.com/artist/6206950/bill-monroe/biography, accessed April 10, 2015.

Thornburgh, Elaine and Logan, Jack. *Music in Our World;* "*Baroque Music*", trumpet.sdsu.edu/M151/logan_M151_MOW.html, accessed May 13, 2015.

Watson, Sonny. *Street Swing.com, "History of the Jig"*. www.streetswing.com/histmain/z3jig.htm, accessed May 7, 2015.

Wood, Jim. "*Fletcher Bright*". Fiddler Magazine, www.fiddle.com/Articlespage?Index=6&ArticleID=18032, accessed April 13, 2015.

CDs and DVDs

Concerto for 2 violins in D Minor BWV 1043 by J.S. Bach,
   "Largo ma non tanto".

DVD: *Oistrakh, Menuhin, Rostropovitch*, EMI video 90450 -
   Classic Archive 2003.

CD: *In Memoriam: Yehudi Menuhin*, Music & Arts 1053.

CD: The Academy of Ancient Music / Christopher Hogwood
   - Jaap Schröder and Christopher Hirons, violin. *Johann
   Sebastian Bach: Violin Concertos Nos. 1 & 2 / Concerto
   for 2 Violins* - Decca / Editions de L'oiseau-Lyre
   B000004CX4 1990.

Old Joe Clark Fiddle Renditions on Youtube.com

Abair, Casey. www.youtube.com/watch?v=0nDWVDkGuSs,
   accessed May 4, 2015.

Bluegrass twin fiddle, All star rendition.
   www.youtube.com/watch?v=QI7i7d4W2U4–, accessed 4
   May, 2015

Fiddle John. www.youtube.com/watch?v=DZw9hB1yNYY,
   accessed April 13, 2015.

Michael. www.youtube.com/watch?v=BVw2NVQ3-L4,
   accessed May 4, 2015.

Rossell, Ole. www.youtube.com/watch?v=fCSKACeycT8,
   accessed May 4, 2015.

Glossary

Sources: *New Harvard Dictionary of Music* (D.M. Randel – editor)
The Encyclopedia of Country Music (P.Kingsbury – editor)
Wikipedia; *The Complete Idiot's Guide to Playing the Fiddle* by Ellery Klein;
Teaching from the Balance Point by Edward Kreitman; *The American Fiddle
Method* by Faith Farr and Brian Wicklund; *Banjo for Dummies*, by Bill
Evans; *Jazz Styles: History and Analysis* by Mark C. Gridley; *Old-Time Fiddle
for the Complete Ignoramus* by Wayne Erbsen; *The Contemporary Violin:
Extended Performance Techniques* by Patricia Strange and Allen Strange

Acoustic	Not electric
Allemande	[Fr., German] A Renaissance and Baroque dance that was cultivated as an independent instrumental piece ca. 1580-1750. It became the first of the four core movements of the solo suite. The Allemande originated in the early or mid-16th century as a "German Dance". It was a fast dance in duple meter often followed by a triple-meter *Nachtanz*. Originating in the mid-18th century, it was a dance in triple meter. It involved the giving of both hands to the partner, from which evolved the American square dance call.
Articulation	In performance, the characteristics of attack and decay of single tones and the means by which these characteristics are produced.

Back beat	A sharp attack on beats two and four of a 4/4 measure, often sounded continuously on the snare drum.
Back-up	Accompaniment (APC)
Banjo	A plucked stringed instrument with a long, fretted neck and a circular body in the form of a shallow, one-headed drum. The five string banjo has four strings (often metal) running the length of the neck plus a shorter fifth string placed next to the lowest string and fastened to a peg at the fifth fret. The most common tunings are g' c g b d' and g' d g b d'. Tenor banjos and plectrum banjos have four strings. The former is tuned c g d' a', the latter d g b e'. Four- string banjos are strummed with a plectrum. Five-string banjos may be plucked with the thumb and forefinger, the thumb and first three fingers, or the thumb and first two fingers. The fifth string serves primarily as a drone. Earl Scruggs, with his virtuoso three-finger style, made the banjo an important instrument in bluegrass music. (New Harvard Dictionary) Open-back folk or old-time banjos may use gut or steel strings. Resonator-backed banjos almost always are steel-strung and are typically used in bluegrass music. (The Encyclopedia of Country music / APC)

Binary form	A movement in binary form contains two parts, each usually repeated. The first generally modulates from the tonic to a related key. In short binary movements there is often no modulation, the first part merely ending with a half cadence. The relationship of the two parts is usually quite close: the thematic material, like the harmony, may be said to be complementary rather than contrasting.
Bluegrass	A style of country and western music brought to prominence in the mid-1940s, first on broadcasts of the grand Ole Opry, by Bill Monroe and his Blue Grass Boys. The term refers to Monroe's native state, Kentucky (the Bluegrass State). Bluegrass is typically performed by a "string band" consisting of a combination of nonelectric instruments such as violin, mandolin, guitar, five-string banjo, and double bass, with some or all of the instrumentalists also singing. Instrumental solos or breaks alternate with the singing, in which the melody occupies a relatively high tessitura and is a second voice from the top when harmonized.
Blue note	In Afro-American music, especially in blues and jazz, the lowered third, seventh, and sometimes fifth scale degrees of the otherwise major scale. The degree of inflection may vary considerably.

Break	A brief, fast-moving, improvised solo. In bluegrass and related styles, an improvised instrumental solo occurring within the framework of an ensemble performance.
Cajun music	Music performed by white musicians and related to Zydeco music: originating among blacks in Cajun Louisiana and combining elements of French Cajun – *Canadian* – traditions with blues, rhythm and blues, rock and roll, Caribbean music, and country and western music. Traditional instruments are the accordion and washboard, to which have been added electric guitar, bass, and drums.
Chin-rest	A holding device for the violin and other bowed stringed instruments played on the arm, allowing the player to grip the instrument firmly between chin and shoulder for ease of left-hand shifting without damping the sound by touching the table of the instrument with the chin. It is usually clamped at the bottom block area to the left of or directly above the tailpiece.
Chop	A percussive bow technique, used in back-up (and solos) in bluegrass music. The bow is thrown vertically onto the strings and quickly pulled up. Originally the chop was made popular by Richard Greene in the 1960s. Later, Darol Anger developed it further, expanding

Chord | its use beyond bluegrass to jazz and other contemporary music styles. (APC)

Chord | Three or more pitches sounded simultaneously; two such pitches are normally referred to as an interval.

Church mode | Church modes were used in the classification of Gregorian chant were formulated by ca. 1000. Eight modes are defined, each according to final (i.e., the pitch on which melodies in that mode end), the intervallic relationship of other pitches to the final, and ambitus (i.e., the range of pitches available from the scale type).

Clawhammer style banjo - A varied banjo playing style and a common component of old-time music. It is primarily a down-picking style. The hand assumes a claw-like shape and the strumming finger is kept fairly stiff, striking the strings by the motion of the hand at the wrist and/ or elbow, rather than a flicking motion by the finger. (Wikipedia, accessed 10/2/15)

Concerto | From the latter part of the 17th century to the present, a multimovement (occasionally multisectional) work for soloist or soloists and orchestra. (fr. It. concertare, to join together. In the 16th through the early 18th centuries, a diverse ensemble of voices, instruments, or both, or a composition for such an ensemble. In the 17th century, the term concerto took on the additional Latin meaning of "fighting" or "contending", referring to the opposition between soloist(s) and orchestra of the modern concerto.

Contra dance / Contredanse (Fr.) A fast dance movement in duple meter (usually simple, but sometimes compound), constructed of a series of repeated eight-measure strains that maintain the simple motivic and textural qualities of dance music.

Courante (Fr.; It. *correntek*) A Baroque dance movement in triple meter. It originated in the 16th century and became a regular member of the solo suite, following the allemande, by ca. 1630. Two versions, ultimately considered French and Italian, coexisted. The Italian type uses fast triple meter (3/4 or 3/8). The mature French courante was described by contemporary theorists as solemn and grave, having the same pulse as a sarabande. It is usually notated in 3/2. Both types are usually in binary form.

Cross-tuning An alternative tuning used for the open strings of a string instrument. The term refers to the practice of retuning the strings. In folk music traditions cross-tunings are used to give the instrument a different sound by altering the pitch of string resonances and drones. (Wikipedia, accessed October 3, 2015)

Down-bow / Up-bow   During the down-bow the hand moves away from the violin; during the up-bow the hand moves toward the violin.

Double stop   The execution of two pitches simultaneously. This is accomplished by means of stopping (i.e., fingering) strings with the left hand in such a way as to allow two pitches to sound simultaneously.

Drone (note)   A long, sustained tone in a piece of music, often intended to imitate the sound of an instrument that plays a constant pitch, usually pitched below the melody.

Dynamics   That aspect of music relating to degrees of loudness.

Etude/Study   A composition designed to improve the technique of an instrumental performer by isolating specific difficulties and concentrating his or her efforts on their mastery. A single etude usually focuses on one technical problem.

Fill   A brief animated solo interpolated between phrases of melody.

415 Hz   The frequency in the International System of Units (SI). It reflects the standard frequency for the pitch (A2 – above the middle C).

Georgia Shuffle   The "Georgia Shuffle" is a two-stroke pattern with a one-note single bow, followed by three slurred or linked notes. This pattern can begin on either the strong or the weak beat of the measure. (The Contemporary Violin:

	Extended Performance Techniques by Patricia Strange and Allen Strange – Scarecrow Press, January 21, 2003)
Gigue	[Fr., fr. Eng. jig; Ger, *Gigue*; It. *giga*; Sp. *giga*, *jiga*]. A fast baroque dance movement in binary form, the last movement of the mature suite. The dance originated in Ireland and England. It was known in France by the 1650s.
Harmony	[fr. Gr., Lat. *harmonia*]. The relationship of tones considered as they sound simultaneously, and the way such relationships are organized in time.
Harmonic structure (of the phrase)	The phrase is the basic unit in which tonality may be established, projected, or changed by means of harmony. A phrase has harmonic structure as much as melodic or rhythmic structure.
Harpsichord	A stringed keyboard instrument in use from the 16th through the 18th century and revived since the 1880s. Each string is plucked by a quill plectrum mounted in the pivoted tongue of a fork-shaped jack that stands at the rear end of the key lever.
Intonation	The degree to which pitch is accurately produced in performance.
Irish fiddling	Like the rest of Irish traditional music tradition, melodies are embellished through forms of ornamentation, such as rolls, trebles, and cuts.

Irish fiddlers use a vocabulary of bow slurs different from other fiddle traditions, at least in proportion of usage. Most notably, fiddlers often slur into the beat to produce a certain lilt, not unlike the Newcastle hornpipe style of bowing in England and Scotland. Slow airs are occasionally played, but the style is best known for fast, snappy reels and jigs. (Wikipedia, accessed 10/3/15)

Jam session   A session where musicians improvise in an informal setting. Jam sessions ordinarily involve changing gatherings of musicians playing for personal pleasure, but some sessions are institutionalized in concerts or on recordings.

Jig   A vigorous dance popular in the British Isles from the 16th century onward. The word seems to come from the French *giguer* (to frolic, to leap).

Key   In tonal music, the pitch relationships that establish a single pitch class as a tonal center or tonic (key note), with respect to which the remaining pitches have subordinate functions. The key of a work is defined in terms of the particular major or minor scale from which its principal pitches are drawn.

Kick-off   How a bluegrass fiddler starts a tune or song. (Old-Time Fiddle for the Complete Ignoramus by Wayne Erbsen / Native Ground Books & Music, Jan 9 2005).

Legato   [It., bound] smooth and connected bow-stroke. (APC).

Lick   A phrase or melodic fragment (Jazz Styles; history and analysis by Mark C. Gridley. Prentice Hall, New Jersey – third edition, 1988).

Martelé   [French] "Hammered" bow-stroke. (APC) / Spiccato [It., strong; marked] bouncing the bow on the strings. (APC) / Legato [It., bound] smooth and connected bow-stroke. (APC).

Meter   The pattern in which a steady succession of rhythmic pulses is organized; also termed time. Most works of Western tonal music are characterized by the regular recurrence of such patterns.

Movement   Any self-contained and thus at least potentially independent section of a larger work such as a sonata, symphony, concerto, string quartet, suite, cantata, oratorio, or even Mass.

Notes inégales [Fr., unequal notes]. A performing convention that renders divisions of the beat in alternating long and short values, even if written in equal values, to add grace or liveliness to the music.

Old-time fiddling   A genre of American folk music. "Old time fiddle tunes" may be played on fiddle, banjo or other instruments but are nevertheless called "fiddle tunes". The genre has European and African origins and traces from the colonization of North America by immigrants from England, France, Germany, Ireland, Scotland as well as slaves brought from west Africa in the 1600s and thereafter. (Wikipedia: Reiner, David; Anick, Peter (2003), *Old-Time Fiddling Across America*, Mel Bay Publications, p. 182, ISBN 978-0-7866-5381-2)

Open-back banjo   Open-back banjos generally have a mellower tone and weigh less than resonator banjos. They also usually have a different setup than a resonator banjo, often with a higher string action (*string action* refers to how high the strings are positioned above the fingerboard). Open-back players use metal, nylon, or gut strings, depending on the style of music they're playing, how their instrument is set up, and the sound they want to get from their banjos. (Banjo for Dummies, by Bill Evans, 2nd edition, January 2014).

Ornamentation   The modification of music, usually but not always through the addition of notes, to make it more beautiful of effective, or to demonstrate the abilities of the interpreter.

Partita   [fr. It. *parte*, part] In the late 16th and 17th century, a variation, usually one on a traditional melody such as *romanesca* or *passomezzo*. In the late Baroque period, a suite. The best-known examples are Bach's solo violin and keyboard partitas.

Phrasing	The realization, in performance, of the phrase structure of a work; the phrase structure itself. The realization of phrase structure is largely a function of the performer's articulation.
Pick	Plectrum; To pluck a stringed instrument, especially a guitar or banjo, rather than strum it; thus to play melodies as well as chords.
Pitch	The perceived quality of a sound that is chiefly a function of its fundamental frequency – the number of oscillations per second (called Hertz, abbr.Hz) of the sounding object or of the particles of air excited by it. In general, pitch is regarded as becoming higher with increasing frequency and lower with decreasing frequency.
Position	In string playing, the location of the hand on the fingerboard. In first or natural position on the violin, the first or index finger stops the pitch o whole tone above the open string, the fourth or little finger reaching a perfect fifth above the open string. Successively higher positions are numbered in order as the first finger is used to stop successively higher pitches of the diatonic scale. A movement from one position to another is termed a shift.
Rhetoric	[fr. Gr. "rhētor", a speaker in the assembly]. In public speaking, the means of effective advocacy; in prose and poetry, the codification of verbal strategies that enhance the reception

	of a text; in music, the conscious, consistent use of patterns and formal arrangements to engender in an audience a sense of aesthetic satisfaction or psychological plausibility that clarifies or heightens the intended effect of a composition or performance.
Rubato	[It. tempo rubato, stolen time]. In performance, the practice of altering the relationship among written note-values and making the established pulse flexible by accelerating and slowing down the tempo.
Sacred Music	Religious music (also sacred music) is music performed or composed for religious use or through religious influence. (Wikipedia, accessed 10/3/2015)
Sarabande	(French). A dance of Spanish origin, mentioned by Cervantes and also by Shakespeare in *Much Ado about Nothing* (1599). Its music is in triple time, with long notes and many ornaments. It begins with the first beat of the measure, and its second beat is very often dotted or tied over to the third. As a stylized dance form it was a regular member of the suite, taking place between the Courante and the Gigue.
Saw strokes	One bow stroke per note. (The American Fiddle Method by Faith Farr and Brian Wicklund, Mel Bay publications, December 17, 2010).
Scale	A collection of pitches arranged in order from lowest to highest or from highest to lowest.

Scratch-in   See: kick off; a rhythmic lead in to a fiddle tune, indicating timing and tempo to back up musicians. A *scratch in* typically is played at the frog end of the bow (APC)

Scordatura   [It., from *scordare*, to mistune]. Unconventional tuning of stringed instruments, particularly lutes and violins, used to facilitate or make available otherwise difficult or impossible pitch combinations, alter the characteristic timbre of the instrument to increase brilliance, reinforce certain sonorities or tonalities by making them available on open strings, imitate other instruments, etc.

Secular Music Music, not associated with or concerned with religion. In the West, secular music developed in the Medieval period and was used in the Renaissance. (Wikipedia, accessed 10/3/15)

Shoulder-rest An accessory that can be found on violins and violas. It may be made of wood, aluminum, carbon fiber or plastic. Usually, the shoulder rest attaches to the edge of the back of the violin with "feet" padded with rubber tubing or made of soft plastic. The goal of a shoulder rest is to allow a more comfortable attitude while playing by adding height to the shoulder and preventing the instrument from slipping. (*Teaching from the Balance Point* by Edward Kreitman, 1998. Western Springs, Illinois,

	60558: Western Springs School of Talent Education).
Shuffle	A combination of the saw stroke and a slurred stroke. The Nashville shuffle is the most basic version. This is a two-beat note (or a two-note slur) followed by two separately bowed notes. (The Complete Idiot's Guide to Playing the Fiddle by Ellery Klein, Penguin 2008).
Slur	A curved line placed above two or more notes of different pitch to indicate that they are to be performed legato. In the case of bowed instruments, this generally means in a single bow.
Sonata	[It.] A work for one or more solo instruments, usually in several movements, and prevalent from the 17th century on. This definition must be refined for each historical period and must allow for exceptions, since the term sonata has at times been used for instrumental works that include a part for a voice or, in the 17th and 18th centuries, for works that could also be performed by orchestra. In the Baroque period, the term sonata was applied in Italy not only to dance collections but also to a new type of instrumental work in an abstract style. Outside Italy, betraying both Italian origins and influence, only this new type was normally called sonata, dance collections being entitled *ordre*, partita, or suite.
Spiccato	[It., strong; marked] bouncing the bow on the strings. (APC)

Spinet	A small harpsichord, almost always with a single keyboard and set of jacks, strung diagonally from left to right with the bass strings at the rear. Spinets were essentially domestic instruments.
Suite	[Fr., succession, following]. A series of disparate instrumental movements with some element of unity, most often to be performed as a single work. The Baroque solo suite came close to having a specific pattern of dance movements at its core, but even then looseness of definition and variability of design were implicit in the term. The origins of the suite are found in dance music pairing two contrasting dances.
Swing	An intangible rhythmic momentum in jazz. Specifically manifested in a variety of relationships between long and short notes, or in the presentation of single notes.
Swing note	A performance practice, mainly in jazz-influenced music, in which some notes with equal written time values are performed with unequal durations, usually as alternating long and short. (Wikipedia, accessed 10/4/15)
Square dance	A folk dance of the U.S. danced by groups of four couples forming a square; also, an occasion on which such dances are danced. The dance itself was derived from the French *quadrille* in the 19th century. It employs music in moderately fast duple meter performed by a fiddle and or various other instruments while the steps are called out to the dancers by a caller.

Tempo	[It., time] The speed at which music is performed, i.e., the rate per unit of time of metrical pulses in performance.
Texas swing music or:	*Western swing music* is a subgenre of American country music that originated in the late 1920s in the West and South among the region's Western string bands. It is dance music, often with an up-tempo beat. The movement was an outgrowth of jazz, and similarities with gypsy jazz are often noted. The music is an amalgamation of rural, cowboy, polka, folk, Dixieland jazz and blues blended with swing. (Wikipedia, accessed 10/4/15)
Triplet	Three notes of equal value to be played in the time normally occupied by two notes of the same value.
Triple time	A musical meter characterized by a *primary* division of 3 beats to the bar, usually indicated by 3 (simple) or 9 (compound) in the upper figure of the time signature. (Wikipedia, accessed 10/4/15)
Up-bow	See: Down bow
Vibrato	[It., from Lat. *vibrare,* to shake]. A slight fluctuation of pitch used by performers to enrich or intensify the sound. In modern string playing, vibrato is produced by rocking the left hand, usually from the wrist, as a note is played.

Viola da gamba   An instrument belonging to the viol family, held between the legs. A forerunner of the cello.

Virginal   A small harpsichord, almost always with one set of strings and jacks and a single keyboard. The strings run at right angles to the keys rather than obliquely as in the spinet. Unlike the spinet, the virginal has its long bass strings at the front.

About the Author

Annemieke Pronker-Coron studied at the Amsterdam Sweelinck Conservatory in her native country, the Netherlands, where her teachers included Jan Henrichs and baroque specialist Jaap Schröder. She also studied music therapy in London. After starting her career in the Netherlands by playing in different orchestral settings and teaching violin, Annemieke went to the United States to do research in bluegrass fiddling. Subsequently she emigrated to Gainesville, Florida.

A former member of the Gainesville Chamber Orchestra, Annemieke teaches violin and fiddle. She is an active promoter of music in the community, having helped inaugurate the Sawgrass Fiddle Contest, the Annasemble and Young Annasemble orchestras under her musical direction. She has taught string programs in local schools, including at the Einstein School for children with learning disabilities.

Annemieke is a member of the Alachua Consort, a baroque-focused trio with oboe and organ and plays electric violin in the Greek band EMBROS. Her research into different musical styles led her to a course in New York City with Mark O'Connor and Pamela Wiley. She now teaches O'Connor's *New American Violin Method.* She lives in Gainesville with her husband Jonathan and son David.

A Note of Appreciation

Over the years many friends, colleagues and family have supported my endeavor to write this book. I thank all for accompanying me on this journey. I would like to extend a special thank you to Dr. Miriam Zach and Dr. Mikesch Muecke for believing in the value of the book and for their guidance and help. I would like to extend a special thank you to Roseanne Russo and Mary Wisnieski for helping edit, to Dr. Howard Coron, my father in law, for his constructive advice, and to my husband Jonathan for standing by me throughout the process.

www.ingramcontent.com/pod-product-compliance
Lightning Source LLC
Chambersburg PA
CBHW070330090426
42733CB00012B/2422